Selling Antiques & Collectibles

50 Ways to Improve Your Business

Selling Antiques & Collectibles

50 Ways to Improve Your Business

DON JOHNSON • ELIZABETH A. BORLAND

WALLACE-HOMESTEAD BOOK COMPANY *Radnor, Pennsylvania*

Published in Radnor, Pennsylvania 19089, by Wallace-Homestead,
a division of Chilton Book Company

Library of Congress Catalog Card No. 92-50675
ISBN 0-87069-685-8

Designed by Adrianne Onderdonk Dudden
Manufactured in the United States of America

1 2 3 4 5 6 7 8 9 0 2 1 0 9 8 7 6 5 4 3

Contents

Introduction

Late one night, long past the bottom of the Doritos bag and halfway through a package of Chips Deluxe, we had a revelation. We could be on to something here.

We were sure of it the next morning when some guy named Bass knocked on the door and flashed a badge. Actually, he had the wrong address. But, that's another story.

Back to the revelation. There really *is* a need for this book.

A number of books provide the uninitiated with an overview of how to become a dealer. But none tackles the specific problems of how to provide good customer service and create effective displays. The industry needs such a book.

"Why customer service?" you ask. Because the antiques industry, like traditional retail markets, can no longer afford to treat customers as disposable entities. Shoppers want to know that they and their business are appreciated. When you reward customers with personal attention, they will reward you with repeat business.

Likewise, dealers can't afford to ignore displays. With the proliferation of antique malls and shops, it's becoming more difficult to stand out in the crowd. Merchandise is no longer enough. You need to court your customer with attractive displays.

While this book will teach you how to create effective displays, we are certainly not advocating that everyone's displays look alike. Our suggestions are just that: suggestions. Work with them. Adapt them to meet your individual needs.

We make no guarantees. We understand that not every suggestion will work for every dealer. Your success with a particular tip will depend on a variety of factors, including geographic location, clientele, and the economy.

Our suggestions are relatively easy to implement. We have tried to include tips that are simple and inexpensive to carry out.

With few exceptions, the examples cited are taken from personal experience. These accounts are not indended to be critical; instead, they are meant to be used as learning tools.

Learn well. And, best of luck with your business.

Acknowledgments

The authors wish to thank the following for their assistance and/or the use of their antiques and collectibles which are featured in several photographs: John Borland; Barry and Barbara Carter; Tom Hoepf; The Illinois Antique Center, Peoria, Illinois; Richard and Phyllis Johnson; the Knightstown Antique Mall, Knightstown, Indiana; New Castle-Henry County Public Library, New Castle, Indiana; Dan Philips; Kurt Schnieders; and Connie Swaim.

I The Basics

Antiques dealers are an integral part of the retail marketplace. There are few differences between selling antiques and selling traditional goods such as sweaters or kitchen appliances. What separates you from more traditional retailers is the unique nature of your business. Still, you face many of the same problems and challenges that confront other merchants.

The antiques market has been besieged by a horde of dealers. Some succeed. Others don't. Many just get by. You, however, want to stand out. You want to separate yourself from the throng. To do so, you must understand and use basic marketing strategies and provide excellent customer service.

Without an understanding of the fundamentals of marketing and customer service, the information contained in the remainder of this book is worthless. The relevance and importance of each tip will only be apparent when you comprehend why its implementation is necessary.

In any business there are two objectives: provide quality products or services, and make money doing so. But, there's a big difference between selling and helping people to buy. That difference is one of attitude.

Traditional selling is rather manipulative. You take what you have and talk somebody into buying it. The emphasis is on making the sale, and success is measured solely on the basis of the day's cash receipts.

On the other hand, helping someone to buy is both a responsive and a creative process. You determine what the customer wants or needs, and you try to match it with merchandise you already have.

Here the concern is for satisfying the customer. The measure of your success is the amount of repeat business generated.

Customers are influenced by the depths of your beliefs and emotions. This is because people are ruled by emotions and emotions are contagious. If you are excited about your merchandise, they will be, too. Nothing can substitute for an enthusiastic belief that the products you offer are the best available.

General Theory of Marketing

"People don't buy goods, they buy solutions to problems. They don't buy ¼-inch drill bits, they buy ¼-inch holes." This well-known marketing axiom highlights the fact that consumers are more likely to purchase items that can be used to solve particular problems or meet specific needs.

Customers don't buy what your shop sells. Rather, they buy what your goods and services do for them. The antiquarian bookseller doesn't sell books; he sells pleasant hours of reading and the benefits of new-found knowledge. The general-line antiques dealer doesn't sell things; he sells good feelings and happy memories.

People buy with emotion. Few of their purchases are actual necessities. They tend to buy what they want, and wants are based on feelings—they need food, but they want steak. However, it's logic that will win and keep your customers. Emotion causes them to buy, but logic keeps them sold and coming back. When you give sound reasons why your products are a good value for the money, your customers will be less likely to regret their purchases.

No discussion of successful marketing is complete without emphasizing the distinction between features and benefits. Features are the physical characteristics of an item. Is it glass or is it china? Will it fit the 11 × 14 picture frame? Features can guarantee the immediate sale if the item is something the customer already desires. Benefits, on the other hand, emphasize what the merchandise can do for the customer. It is important to drive home the fact that the product can improve or enhance his life.

Unfortunately, many dealers adopt a passive approach to selling their wares. They rely on interested customers and die-hard collectors to buy their merchandise. Such short-sightedness overlooks those casual shoppers

A Matter of Semantics

People love to buy but hate to be sold.

Consider your elegant Lalique Thistles vase displayed on the mantel. Did someone sell you that vase? No. You cleverly spotted it at a flea market and are quite proud of yourself for buying it.

Now, assume you discover the vase is a fake. Did you still buy it? No. Some fast-talking con artist tricked you into purchasing a bill of goods.

As consumers, we gladly take all credit for the purchase we are proudest of, but we are quick to blame the seller when we feel short-changed.

not searching for specific items. Creative selling techniques can motivate these shoppers to buy. To encourage them to make a purchase, speak to them directly and personally. Use "you" language to show them you understand their needs.

There is a middle ground between apathy and hard-sell tactics. A simple smile and friendly greeting may cause a browser to buy from you rather than a competitor.

One of the keys to effective marketing is to lengthen the amount of time the customer spends with your merchandise. Keeping him in your booth or shop for as long as possible increases your chance of making a sale. But, encouraging him to stay will only be successful if he is happy, comfortable, and at ease.

Dealers who talk to themselves can be rather daunting for the customer. Likewise, dealers who give the impression that patrons are intruding encourage them to hustle out the door. Considerate dealers help customers feel at home by providing a pressure-free environment in which to examine the merchandise.

People tend to spend their money where and when they feel good. In other words, customers only buy when they are feeling positive about you and your products. Never burden customers with your problems. Doing so makes them sad, and sad people only buy at funeral homes. Instead, put yourself in a positive emotional state. Feelings are contagious, and people will buy when they are happy.

Likewise, encourage customers to tell you about only those problems you can solve for them. The broad question, "How are you?" can prompt a discussion of the fact that their daughter is in prison and the IRS just seized their bank account. A more upbeat greeting such as "Good to see you again!" can keep the conversation focused on pleasant thoughts.

Successful marketing does not take place only at the time of the sale. The way you say hello and goodbye offers a chance for you to single out each customer. Greet shoppers with a warm smile and make eye contact. Call them by name if possible. Friendly greetings are effective word-of-mouth marketing. Every moment you're with the customer is a potential marketing opportunity. Use this time to solidify your relationship and provide better service.

Keep in mind that what happens after the sale is of equal importance in creating a loyal customer base. Know what you'll do if the customer is not satisfied. A clear policy can convert disgruntled customers into satisfied individuals who will return to do business.

Customer Service

SOCIETY IS ALWAYS TAKEN BY SURPRISE AT ANY NEW EXAMPLE OF COMMON SENSE.

—*Ralph Waldo Emerson*

It is impossible to overstate the importance of customer service. Good service wins customers, the lack of it loses customers; it is one of the top considerations when selecting a business from which to buy.

Trying to compete solely on the basis of product or price is insufficient. Distinguish yourself on the basis of service superiority. Attention to the customer is the standard by which you will be judged. Service is not a competitive edge, it is *the* competitive edge.

Be responsive to the needs of your customer. You should be accessible, available, and willing to help when he has a problem. Be empathetic. Put yourself in his shoes. Listen intently, ask the right questions, and tailor your responses to meet his needs. Don't treat him the way you want to be treated. Instead, treat him as he wants to be treated.

Using superior customer service to produce the kind of repeat business on which success depends is not a one-shot deal. It demands a day-by-day, minute-by-minute dedication to preserving high standards.

Future behavior is largely based on the consequences of past and present behavior. If the results are rewarding, odds are great that the behavior will be repeated. Simply, you get more of the behavior you reward. As a dealer, your very livelihood depends on rewarding the customer. When a customer or potential customer visits, telephones, or has some contact with your business, he will experience certain consequences of his action. The more he feels rewarded, the greater the chance is that he will spend money and the greater the odds are that he will continue to be your customer.

Damning a Sale

Refrain from using language that some customers might find offensive. At one outdoor antique show, two women were looking at hats in a display of vintage clothing. "Please try that large hat on. I'm dying to see someone in it," the dealer said. "They look like hell on me!"

The Customer Service Quiz

What you say to your customers can make or break a sale. Rude or off-hand comments can send your customers toward the front door rather than the cash drawer.

Take the following quiz. The incidents described actually occurred. For each, try to choose the response made by the dealer:

1 A customer browsing through a single-owner shop asked, "How much are your three round oak tables?" The dealer replied:

- **a** "I'm sorry. Those are sold. I was just getting ready to move them. However, I do have another table in the next room."
- **b** "I'm sorry. I just brought those in and was getting ready to price them. They're $400 apiece."
- **c** "Do ya wanna know because they aren't priced?"

2 A customer browsing at an antique show asked a dealer, "How much is your Wallace Nutting print?" The dealer replied:

- **a** "I'm sorry. That's not for sale. It's part of a display. However, there's a similar print in the next booth."
- **b** "I'm sorry. It's on hold. The tag must have fallen off. Did you see the other Nutting I have for sale?"
- **c** "It's $48. It oughta' be worth that."

3 A customer walked into an antiques mall. The dealer greeted him with:

- **a** "Hello! Let me know if I can help you with anything."
- **b** "Good afternoon. Feel free to browse. Please let me know if you have any questions."
- **c** "Are you looking for something specific or are you just wasting time?"

In each case, the answer actually given was "C." That, however, does not make it the correct answer. "C" shows a disregard for the customer's feelings and concerns. Take care to avoid these types of responses.

Bonus question: What would have been the better response? Go to the head of the class if you picked "A" or "B."

Read 'em and Weep

"Look and handle but be neat about it."—sign on a box filled with hankies

"If you can't be neat, be gone."—sign taped to a basket of doilies and table covers

Your signs speak for you in your absence. The examples given above spoke volumes about the attitudes of two dealers. You wouldn't intentionally insult a shopper; make sure your signs don't either.

The service problems that drive people away are primarily caused by carelessness, rudeness, and incompetence. Although such behaviors may simply be a matter of apathy or inattention, they can be prevented with a little time and effort.

Perception is the key to providing good customer service. You may have the most efficient, dedicated employees in the world. You can care more about your customers than seems humanly possible. You can stay awake at

> **FYI**
>
> Ways to improve your customer service:
>
> **1** Keep noise down. If you must use a radio, television, or police scanner, keep volume to a minimum.
>
> **2** Read with discretion. That book, magazine, or newspaper you are looking at may give customers the impression your reading material is more important than they are.
>
> **3** Ask the right questions. Asking "What do you collect?" limits the range of items you can show the customer. Try saying, "If I can help you in any way, please let me know," or asking, "Is there anything in particular you were looking for that you didn't find?" Maybe that customer was looking for Dedham dinnerware but didn't see your rabbit platter.
>
> **4** Count back change. It's a dying art. Counting change is a simple way of showing your customer you are concerned about his money and aren't taking his purchase for granted. Except for saying goodbye, this is your last encounter with the buyer. Make it a memorable one.
>
> **5** Put customers at ease. Shadowing them from room to room will make them uncomfortable. Customers don't like to feel as if they are being watched. Give them some space, but let them know you are there to provide assistance when needed.
>
> **6** Be genuine. Greet every person who walks into your shop or booth. *Never* ignore a customer. If someone needs assistance while you are busy with another patron, acknowledge their need with, "I'll be with you as soon as I can." When a customer feels you don't know he is there and/or don't care, you will probably lose his business.
>
> **7** Make patrons comfortable. If possible, provide restrooms and a drinking fountain or soda machine for customers to use. Happy, comfortable customers will be more likely to buy your merchandise.
>
> **8** Foster relationships. Treat each customer as someone special and unique. Customers shop where they are appreciated.
>
> **9** Keep it to yourself. No matter how amusing or dimwitted their actions may have seemed, don't discuss customers in front of other customers. Your present customers will wonder what you say about them once they are gone.
>
> **10** Eat with discretion. If you must eat in front of your customers, keep your activity as inconspicuous as possible. That chili dog you're eating for lunch might remind your customer how hungry he is, sending him out of your booth in search of sustenance. When finished, remove sacks, napkins, condiment containers, half-eaten food, drinks, etc.

night thinking up better ways to serve them. But, until the customer is aware of the fact that you are taking very special care of him and giving him his money's worth, you're wasting your time. It's not the quality of service that you give but the quality of service the customer *perceives* that influences him to buy and come back.

Perceived service quality is the difference between what the customer actually gets and what he expected to get. Every customer who enters your booth or shop does so with certain expectations about the quality of your goods and the over-all experience of doing business with you. When you don't meet his expectations, he perceives the service quality as relatively low; when you exceed his expectations, he perceives the quality as high.

When problems do arise, don't avoid them. Use them as opportunities to demonstrate the great service you give. Suppose you sell a Maxfield Parrish print to a customer who comes back two weeks later and is unhappy because it doesn't match the new dining room wallpaper. Most dealers in this situation would adopt a tough-luck attitude. They'd keep the money, but they'd probably lose the customer.

You can turn this problem to your advantage. Remind yourself that arguing with the customer will accomplish little. Instead, generate some goodwill by providing special, personal consideration. Make an honest effort to find a mutually satisfactory solution. Break the rules if you have to. Resolve the matter in a congenial rather than an argumentative tone.

In the long run, your reputation is one of your most valuable assets. No one sale is important enough to jeopardize that. Do what it takes to ensure that the customer is satisfied. Happy customers are repeat customers; and repeat customers are future business.

Dealer Attitude and Knowledge

Think of yourself as an advertisement for your shop or mall. Remember that first impressions can make the difference between getting and not getting the sale. Dress conservatively and conduct yourself in a businesslike manner. You want to attract respect, not attention.

Remember, customers don't just see you while you are working the shop floor or ringing up sales at the cash register. You may also be seen while you are doing paperwork in your office or when you are picking up trash in your parking lot. Be presentable and amiable in every circumstance.

First impressions are based on more than just physical appearance. Emotions must also be considered. Enthusiasm is contagious. If you are enthusiastic about your merchandise, your customer will be enthused as well. Display indifference, and so will he.

Respect for yourself and your merchandise must be apparent to the customer. Be cheerful, but not overly so. Be sincere and you'll be taken sincerely. Know your inventory so well that there is not one question you can't answer or find the answer for.

Dealer attitude when finalizing the sale can determine whether the customer leaves with a good impression and whether he will return. Show some appreciation. Thank the customer for his purchase. For those shoppers who do not buy anything, thank them for taking the time to visit your shop.

Acknowledge every customer, especially when that customer first addresses you. If the customer says "Thank you" as he is leaving, you had better say more than "Uh huh." Such a half-hearted response tells your

Loose Lips Sink Sales

Be careful what you say. Someone may be listening.

That someone may be a potential customer. But he'll be a lost customer if he thinks you will take advantage of him.

At one mall, a dealer was bragging about his good fortune. While at another shop, he had spotted an art pottery lamp tagged $35. The shop owner accepted his offer of $20. The dealer then priced the lamp $95 and put it in his mall, where it immediately sold.

Although the dealer did nothing wrong, his actions could be construed as ruthless and greedy. A customer who overhears the tale may avoid his booth.

customer that you are not interested in him and really don't care whether he ever visits your shop again.

At the very least your response should be, "Thank you for stopping. Come back again." Better yet, take advantage of the opportunity and promote your shop and your merchandise. Follow your closing with, "We're bringing in merchandise all the time, so check back with us."

Problem resolution is probably the most difficult aspect of customer service. You can react defensively or helpfully. Which response you choose will have profound results on repeat business.

The problem of an irate customer is really two problems in one: first, you must decide how to deal with the customer's feelings; then you must figure out how to solve the problem that made him mad in the first place. If you solve the problem but make no attempt to soothe the anger, the customer probably won't return. People don't shop where they don't feel good.

The first step in dealing with an upset customer's feelings is to keep cool. Don't argue. If you make him look foolish, you'll lose a customer. If you allow him to make you look foolish, he'll think you're a push-over, and he won't want to buy from you. Going on the defensive is a lose–lose proposition.

Take the offensive with a positive approach. When a customer is critical or complains, don't take it personally. In the process, he is also providing you with information. Listen with empathy for the clues you need to help him solve his problem.

Avoid treating the problem as if it's routine. That's just asking for trouble. Your customer's problem is unique and deserves individual treatment and attention.

When you offer solutions, state them positively. Tell your customer what you *can* do rather than what you *can't* do. "I'll deliver your Seller's cabinet first thing tomorrow morning" rather than "I can't make the delivery today."

Bring the incident to a polite close by asking, "Is there any other way I can be of help to you today?" If there is not, thank him for telling you his concerns. A customer with the passion to get angry also has the ability to be loyal. You might even want to solidify the positive resolution by making a follow-up call. Double-check that the problem has been taken care of to the customer's satisfaction. This reminds him that his business is important to you.

Dealer knowledge is equally important as dealer attitude when creating a lasting, positive impression. Other things, such as financial resources, being equal, knowledgeable dealers will succeed. Knowledge is power. Understanding your merchandise gives you confidence, and that confidence will win respect and patronage from your customers.

You must know far more about your product than the average person. Why? Because customers will turn to you for answers. They will expect you to be an expert on your subject and will come to you with their questions. Without answers, you will lose credibility, referrals, and future sales.

Prepare for customers' questions by having the answers before they ask. Customers evaluate the competence of a business largely on the basis of how much the workers appear to know. Develop a list of things to find out about every product you work with. What is it? What does it do? When was it made? Who manufactured it?

Know your merchandise, what you paid for it, and what you are willing to sell it for. Do you know what your bottom line is on every piece in your stock? Do you know the lowest price you'll take, no matter what the circumstance? If your responses are "no," you'd better find the answers. You should be able to give your customers timely, thoughtful replies to such questions.

If a customer has to ask about the price of an item, be sure you have an immediate answer. Making the customer wait gives him time to think. He may decide that you don't know your merchandise or, worse yet, that you don't care.

Particularly in the retail trade, reputation is extremely important. The dealer who, over a period of years, sells merchandise at reasonable prices and deals fairly with his clients will develop a following.

II The Market

Individuals are influenced by a variety of factors that affect their buying decisions. Understand those factors and you begin to understand your customer. Once you understand your customer, you begin to know your buyer.

This is not an easy task. Deciphering the list of possible influences can seem like an endless chore. Your customer's buying decisions may be affected by his income as well as by his interests. Whether a blue-collar worker or an executive, a sports buff or a needlework aficionado, it will determine the type of merchandise he is interested in.

Your customer's age and his activities can also affect whether or not he will buy certain merchandise. Someone who is 15 will obviously have different spending habits than does someone who is 50. Likewise, avid readers will be interested in antiquarian books, and gardeners will be interested in floral prints.

Profiling your customers is not just a matter of determining what they will buy. Sometimes it's a matter of what they won't buy. You shouldn't expect to sell owl collectibles to a logger who has just lost his job because of environmental concerns. Along the same lines, you wouldn't sell wildlife trophies to an animal-rights activist.

1 Consider Demographics

UNDERSTAND YOUR CUSTOMERS; KNOW YOUR BUYERS.

Imagine the roar of hundreds of rumbling stomachs. It's lunch time at the convention. Ravenous businessmen hurry to the food court.

The vendor at the pork chop stand is prepared. He barbecued pork chops all morning. They look fantastic. They smell wonderful. The price is great. Yet all those hungry people pass his stand, opting for pizza or tacos or fruit salads. Still smiling, the undaunted pork salesman waits for his first customer, chops at the ready.

Finally, a puzzled man approaches the vendor. "Why are you selling pork?" he asks. "This is a convention of Jewish businessmen."

"I know," the vendor replies, "But sooner or later the right buyer will come along."

"The right buyer will come along." Some dealers stake their business on just such an uncertainty. The right buyer *will* come along . . . eventually. But the likelihood of finding that buyer increases greatly when you replace the "chance" factor with calculated marketing that specifically targets the customer. You have to ensure that the individual walking through your door will be interested in your merchandise. How do you do this? Know demographics.

Demographics are statistics that describe people. Age, sex, income, education, and religion are all demographic factors which can affect consumers' buying habits. These characteristics can be used to profile your

"At ease!"

You can't underestimate the importance of feeling comfortable in the retail environment.

One dealer in a strip mall was plagued with teenagers lounging outside the shop or riding skateboards. When they were on the sidewalk, traffic in and out of the shop decreased dramatically. Most affected were the elderly, who refused to cross their path. They perceived the teens to be a threat, even though they actually meant no harm.

The dealer expressed his concerns to the teens, asking them to skate and socialize at a park down the street. Once the youngsters were no longer congregating outside the shop, creating a "barrier," the dealer's customers were again comfortable.

Only when you understand the concerns of your customers can you provide what they are seeking—whether it's an Empire chest of drawers they've been looking for or just a quiet place to spend the afternoon.

customers, allowing you to offer merchandise most likely to appeal to them.

For instance, your 1940s "I Want You!" recruiting poster picturing Uncle Sam might be a great item at a wonderful price, but it's going to hang on your wall for months if your customers are more interested in Victorian furniture than they are in World War II memorabilia or poster art. You'll be more likely to sell the poster if your clientele includes service veterans than if many of your shoppers are newlyweds furnishing a first home.

The better you are at precisely defining the customer you are serving, the easier it is to provide the merchandise they are interested in. For instance, if the majority of your customers are over 60, you would expect them to purchase a French Limoges tea set rather than a Melmac picnic ensemble. Likewise, they would be more apt to buy a Zenith cathedral radio than to purchase a Snoopy transistor.

When your merchandise is geared toward a certain segment of the population, those individuals will realize that you are genuinely interested in serving them. Providing your customers with more personal service causes them to feel good about your merchandise and also about themselves. By helping your patrons feel important, you encourage them to return. And repeat customers are the backbone of any successful business.

Using demographic information can also help you to predict trends. Consider baby boomers: they continue to define what is collectible. Having grown up during the advent of the fast-food restaurant, they led the search for premiums and give-aways from those establishments. What once was a relatively obscure field of collecting has fast become a highly competitive market. Blessed were the dealers who recognized the importance of catering to the tastes of baby boomers. They capitalized on the birth of a new collectible by being able to predict what would interest the boomers.

Demographics are great, but the problem is you can't simply go to the library and find a book that tells you everything you need to know about your customers. It doesn't work that way. Demographics vary widely, not only from one area of the country to another, but even on different sides of the street. Accurately determining the demographic characteristics of your clientele requires some research.

Research doesn't necessarily have to involve book work, though. You can learn a lot just from studying your customers. This is easiest if you have an established location, such as an antique mall or shop, from which to operate. Spend time there. Ask yourself questions. Are the shoppers wearing business suits or work uniforms? Are they driving BMWs or pickup trucks? Are those vehicles from surrounding counties or from out of state?

FYI

Helpful sources of demographic information:

1. Area merchants
2. Chamber of Commerce
3. Local business organizations
4. Private Industry Council
5. *Rand McNally Business Atlas*

Note not only what these customers are buying, but what they are interested in and what they are not interested in. What do they stop and look at? Glassware? Furniture? Toys? Be specific. Are those toy collectors looking for cast-iron Arcade firetrucks or Fisher-Price pull toys?

You should also ask the mall or show manager about the dealers who shop there. Where are they from, and what are they looking for? Dealers who want further insight into mall clientele should ask the manager if they can work for a short period of time, anywhere from a few days to a few weeks. You might not realize just how popular Depression glass is until you write a dozen sales receipts in just one weekend. You could also learn that those buyers are taking home only specific patterns, such as Cherry Blossom, or that they prefer particular colors, such as green, or that they are looking for only certain pieces, such as breakfast sets.

Your customers should not only determine what you sell, but where you sell it from. If the majority of your customers are retired, you may be discouraging traffic by locating your shop on the second floor of a building that doesn't have an elevator. Likewise, the general location of your establishment will greatly affect the number of shoppers you attract. Does heavy traffic limit access to your site? Is parking adequate and convenient? Do customers feel safe in your neighborhood?

Every bit of information you learn about your customers will help you to better profile who they are and what they need or want.

2 Learn from Other Dealers

THE BEST IDEAS ARE COMMON PROPERTY.

—*Lucius Annaeus Seneca*

It's hard to say who Seneca stole that thought from. Not that it really matters. He was right. Of course, this first-century philosopher wasn't talking specifically about merchandising antiques and collectibles, but the gist of the matter still applies. Many good ideas are free for the taking. All that's required is a little observation and adaptation.

It's tough being an antiques dealer. There are no manuals outlining how to fold flap A into slot B to create the instantly successful business. Although most how-to books offer some helpful suggestions, they don't provide all the answers. The most important insights will have to come from you, through first-hand observation and on-the-job experience.

Visit other shops, malls, and shows and take notes on the displays and prices. Look at the methods other dealers use to merchandise their goods and incorporate the best ideas into your own displays.

What do you observe? The number-one rule of observation is to examine everything. Don't just look for the good ideas; look for the bad ones, too. You need to know what works and what doesn't. One dealer's Royal Ruby glassware on a white shelving unit may be particularly eye-catching. Another's clear glassware may be lost in the murky depths of a low, dark shelf. By scrutinizing these two groupings, you gain insights useful for planning and creating more effective displays.

Antique shows provide an excellent opportunity for observing a variety of display techniques. Take a clinical look at how dealers set up their booths. Where do they put specific items and why? Is there enough room for show-goers to move about comfortably? Is the lighting adequate? Are items easily accessible? Is the merchandise priced, and are those tags clearly visible?

Do more than simply ask questions in your head. Take notes about what you like and don't like; make sketches when appropriate. If you especially like the way a dealer added lights under a table to highlight blue-decorated stoneware on the floor, draw a diagram. If you are impressed with the overall appearance of a particular booth, note the types of lights used, the color of the table covers, the width of the aisles, etc. File these notes for later reference.

Shows serve as a barometer of the market, highlighting items which are in demand. Item placement itself should tell you something about the

Adaptation is the Name of the Game

Many successful corporate leaders built their companies around the simplest of observations and adaptations.

Clarence Birdseye happened to be in the right place to observe what the Eskimos had known for centuries: quick freezing is a natural process of preservation.

Look at what the late Sam Walton did in building his Wal-Mart empire. An aggressive and outspoken entrepreneur, he turned the retail industry on its ear with his dream of opening a chain of discount stores. Interestingly enough, Mr. Walton's early training came as a manager trainee for J.C. Penney. It was Penney's concept of how to succeed—considering customer satisfaction more important than profit—that he would later borrow and use so effectively.

Although Wal-Mart and Birds Eye Frozen Foods are not related to the field of antiques and collectibles, the stories behind these successful business ventures should serve as inspiring examples for dealers. Observation and adaptation can be put to use by any businessman.

market. Desirable merchandise will be prominently displayed, while other items will be relegated to less visible spots. Vintage baseball gloves were all the rage last year and were individually highlighted at the fronts of tables and in special displays. Now, they are thrown together in a basket that is shoved under a table.

Observe more than just the displays. Look for trends and note prices. Is there a passel of Western memorabilia being offered? That might indicate cowboys and Indians are still popular. Once you know what's available, look at the prices. Steady or increasing prices usually denote continued interest. Low prices might signal that a trend is dying and dealers are dumping their merchandise. Accurately reading these clues can help you decide whether to showcase your Hopalong Cassidy lamp or mark it down.

Observation, however, accomplishes nothing without adaptation and implementation. All those wonderful ideas you've borrowed won't do you a bit of good if they simply remain ideas in your head or notes in a filing cabinet. You must use them.

Change your display of glassware to capitalize on your new-found knowledge that Royal Ruby shows up best against a light-colored background. Add lighting to accent merchandise in shadows. Create a display of Western memorabilia to take advantage of the growing demand for those items. Adaptations might be as extensive as completely restructuring your booth or as minimal as changing the position of two items on a shelf. The amount of work involved isn't important; it's the principle that counts.

3 Learn from Traditional Retailers

COMMIT A NEW KIND OF SHOPLIFTING.

Dust off your fedora and find your trench coat. It's time to go to work. This is a job for you—private eye, dealer-detective. There's a city out there calling your name. Somewhere beyond the bustling streets and neon lights are the clues to help you to solve this caper. You've been on hundreds of cases, but none as important as this.

You open your desk drawer and take out your piece—a ball-point pen nestled inside a pocket-sized notebook. A tug on the fedora, and you're off. It isn't the glamorous job your mother envisioned, but you were never doctor or lawyer material. Here you're in your element. Walking the aisles of department stores and rubbing elbows with sales clerks in gift shops is where you belong. Nothing equals the thrill of gathering information, building your case, so there isn't a thing you don't know when you return to your office.

You're ferreting out the secrets of the retail market, and you're about to use them to your advantage. You've gone undercover to determine how the Hallmarks and Penneys and Marshall-Fields of the world make their stores appealing to their customers. You're out to discover how traditional retailers dress up their displays, how they promote their merchandise, and how they entice their customers to buy.

When your assignment is done, when you take off your trench coat and fedora, when you trade your notebook for a business card that says "antiques," you're ready to implement the techniques you've gathered. You'll be ready for the next customer who walks through *your* door because your displays will look just as good as those created by the traditional retailers in town.

Why should an antiques dealer go to all this trouble?

Traditional retail stores offer some of the best merchandising ideas. They have to. Theirs is a highly competitive market where sales are won and lost based on the shopper's impression of the store and the merchandise. Displays catch the customer's eye. Displays promote sales. Displays make the difference between profit and loss, between having an anniversary sale or having a "Going Out Of Business" sale.

Shop around for ideas and then implement the best. Don't limit yourself to stores that only sell the same types of merchandise you do. Displays used by other businesses might contain ideas you normally wouldn't have

Be a Comparison Shopper

Every trip to the store should be a learning experience. Looking for display ideas is no different than shopping for a new refrigerator or hiring a contractor to side your house. You collect information, make comparisons, and determine which product or service is the best one for the money. In putting together a display, you draw off of the best ideas you have found and implement those which will most effectively showcase your merchandise and promote sales.

thought of. Furniture stores use inviting room settings to sell their merchandise. Major housewares departments can provide suggestions for grouping kitchen accessories.

Take advantage of the ingenuity and expertise of traditional retailers. Note the types of merchandise being offered, whether that business is a small specialty shop or part of a large chain. What product lines are carried? What are the obvious consumer buying trends? If birds are the latest retail phenomenon, highlight your Stangl parrot, Cuckoo board game, and French's bird seed tin.

Additionally, many of the display techniques used by the more traditional retailers can be adopted by antiques dealers. If you are impressed with the arrangement of a shelf of bells in a Hallmark store or intrigued by a football theme promoting athletic wear at Sears, adapt the technique so it can be used with your merchandise. If you see a particularly attractive display of towels at J.C. Penney, borrow the idea for your Irish linens.

Do more than just observe the merchandise and the displays, however. Pay attention to the overall appearance of the store. Are the displays neat and organized? Do you feel crowded, or are you at ease? Are the floors clean? Even the customer's perception of the housekeeping department can influence sales. Determine what it is that makes you comfortable in traditional retail stores and mimic that environment in your booth or mall.

Additionally, traditional retailers pay close attention to outside factors that can influence sales, and they change their merchandise and displays in response to those factors. You should do likewise. The economy, the time of year, and the latest trends affect the antiques industry in the same ways they do the traditional retail market.

You can also learn a lot about customer service by watching the traditional retailers in action. Are they pleasant to their customers or do they not even acknowledge them? Are they genuinely thankful for their business or do they seem indifferent? Do they resolve problems quickly and courteously or does the customer's complaint not really seem to matter? Watch the ways traditional retailers interact with their customers and focus on adapting the positive aspects of this relationship to your own business. Remember, successful businesses are based on repeat customers. Do what it takes to convince the shopper to return.

4 Recognize Environmental, Social, and Historical Concerns

VALUES ARE MORE THAN JUST PRICES.

It's the policy of one local newspaper not to publish photographs of dead mammals. If you bag a 12-point buck during muzzle-loading season, don't expect the paper to run a photo of you and Bambi. Their policy also covers squirrels, rabbits, and the like. If it's a mammal and it's dead, it's off limits.

Catch a stringer of fish, and they'll run red lights to get a photographer down to the dock. Bring in a mushroom larger than your fist, and they'll send you extra copies of the paper when the photo is published. But, dare to mention posing with some lifeless, heretofore warm-blooded, live-bearing creature, and they'll turn a cold shoulder. "Policy," they'll mutter as they walk away.

That policy was developed years ago after numerous complaints from readers offended by photos of hunters with their trophies. The newspaper gave in when enough subscribers banded together and said, "Print any more of those photos, and we'll stop buying your newspaper."

We all have personal value systems that affect what we will or will not buy. Some people won't buy disposable razors. Some won't buy cosmetics tested on animals. Others won't buy anything manufactured outside the United States.

These values are based on environmental, social, and historical concerns that influence consumer spending. As a dealer, awareness of these concerns enables you to offer merchandise your customers will feel comfortable purchasing.

The current movement toward environmental awareness is probably the best example of a value system at work. A throw-away society is no longer acceptable. Earth-friendly products and recycling have become the norm.

Don't wait for environmentally conscious consumers to decide that glass refrigerator storage dishes are an ecological alternative to plastic wrap and aluminum foil. Show them. Highlight refrigerator dishes, incorporating shelf-talkers into the display to underscore the idea.

Emphasizing the features and benefits of these dishes provides a solution to the customer's problem at the same time that it lessens any hesitancy on his part to purchase the item. Not only are you presenting merchandise that is useful, but you are also managing to address your shopper's concern—the wastefulness of wraps and foils.

Refrigerator dishes can be promoted as practical alternatives to disposable foils and wraps. Grouped together with a shelf-talker, these dishes will appeal to "green" consumers.

Besides environmental concerns, social issues can also affect consumer spending. The selling of ethnic items such as black memorabilia comes most readily to mind. Although this category is considered a legitimate collectible by many, others are offended by the stereotyped images.

Dealers who carry this type of merchandise need to be aware that some shoppers are highly offended by such items, which can result in lost sales. Do what you can to lessen the impact. One possible solution is a sign stating that black memorabilia is a legitimate collectible, and that it is being sold purely as a business venture. Although this disclaimer will not influence customers to buy these products, your tacit acknowledgment of their concern may prevent them from deciding to boycott your booth.

Value systems can also be influenced by historic events. This was clearly demonstrated during the Persian Gulf War. Not only did interest in vintage military items increase, but the sale of patriotic collectibles also skyrocketed. Keep abreast of current events and understand that they can influence public sentiment and buying habits.

Historical events, such as the death of a celebrity, can also boost sales. That's what happened following the death of Theodore Geisel, the beloved Dr. Seuss. Collector interest intensified, increasing both demand and prices

▶ FYI

Examples of consumer concerns:

1. Environmental issues—antiques as earth-friendly products
2. Extinction—products made from ivory and scrimshaw
3. Animal rights—animal trophies and skins
4. Ethnic items—black collectibles and Native American issues
5. Public sentiment—"Buy American" theme
6. Historical events—new markets in Eastern Europe
7. Current events—elections and anniversaries
8. Reproductions—fakes, forgeries and fantasy items

for Seuss memorabilia. Dealers who had such items were smart to highlight these pieces immediately after the Good Doctor's death.

When you are aware of the value systems of your customers, you can offer merchandise that is more likely to appeal to them. Keep in mind, people shop from the heart. You might love that new cherry-red Porsche 944, but you know that it makes more sense, both realistically and financially, for you to buy a used Ford Escort wagon. Likewise, value systems will influence the choices your customers make.

5 Respond to the Economy and the Season

HEADLINES AND DATELINES AFFECT BOTTOM LINES.

Sometimes it helps to have a nose for news. If one dealer only had known that, he wouldn't have gone out of business. That dealer and his merchandise are now history. He was last seen lugging a massive oak table to his panel van. He wasn't delivering the table; he was taking it home or hauling it to an auction. His sales weren't enough to cover rent every month. The business failed.

Who knows what the dealer blamed the failure on. The location? The clientele? The weather? Yet, the finger of blame should have been pointed at himself. He didn't do his homework. He failed to realize that merchandise won't always sell itself. His only concern was for putting the table in the mall and slapping a price tag on it. By assuming it would be gone in a day or a week or a month, he counted on sales that never came.

He didn't stop to think that certain items would sell better than others during particular times of the year or under specific economic conditions. You can learn from the mistakes of this unfortunate dealer. A nose for news—reading business publications and following the local economy—can help you to understand the basics of retail sales.

Sales are seldom constant. They fluctuate from day to day, season to season, year to year. Most of the variation is related to the economy or the time of year and, as such, can be anticipated. Your job is to determine what types of merchandise will sell during a strong economy and what will sell during a weak economy. Likewise, you must understand that particular times of the year can also greatly affect consumer spending. Vacations, Christmas, and tax time will all have an impact.

Prepare for these periods by adapting your inventory and displays to compensate for changing conditions. When you understand how the econ-

> **FYI**
>
> Economic factors affect the following:
>
> 1. Volume of sales
> 2. Quality of items sold
> 3. Practicality of items sold
> 4. Investment potential
> 5. Price range people will buy from
> 6. Number of items per sale
> 7. Impulse buying

omy and certain times of the year influence sales, you can use that information to your benefit.

Both the economy and the time of year will have their greatest impact on the volume of sales and the types of merchandise customers are buying. You can expect sales to be good when the local economy is strong. However, if a major manufacturer in your area has been on strike for 15 months, overall sales will naturally decrease. And, a greater proportion of the remaining sales will be utilitarian items. Consumers concerned about money are more likely to buy a drop-leaf table or a set of McKee nested measuring cups than an object which is purely ornamental, such as a Hummel figurine.

Summer is an especially promising time for dealers. Pleasant weather encourages people to be out and about, whether visiting an antique mall or outdoor show. The resulting increase in traffic will consist of both regular customers and new customers, many of whom will be vacation travelers. Dealers searching for inventory to restock their own shelves during the summer months will also account for some of the increase in traffic.

Know what affects your shopper's buying habits. He will probably be more frugal at tax time or during a slow economy than he would be at Christmas.

Seasonal events such as festivals, fairs, and other local attractions can boost sales by increasing traffic through your shop or mall. Cater to those new customers. Highlight any merchandise related to the event. If you are located in the Indianapolis area, spotlight Indy 500 memorabilia during May. If your local chamber of commerce is sponsoring an Oktoberfest, highlight German items.

The type of merchandise sought by your customers will also change with the seasons. You can expect to sell sleds in the winter and garden furniture in the summer. Likewise, sports-related items will be most popular during their respective seasons.

Holidays such as Christmas, Easter, and Halloween will also increase demand for specific items. Showcase your glass ornaments, chalkware bunnies, and papier mâché jack-o-lanterns to capitalize on the holiday spirit.

Tax time can also affect sales. Consumers concerned with making payments to the IRS may curtail spending at the beginning of the year. On the other hand, those receiving refunds may spend some of that money in your shop.

One factor often overlooked when analyzing sales is the impact weather can have. If it's too hot or too cold, people are less likely to be out shopping. Also, the terms hot and cold do not just refer to conditions outside your establishment. If your shop or mall is drafty and cool in the winter or muggy and hot in the summer, customers will not want to spend a lot of time there.

6 Read Trade and General-Interest Publications

READING HABITS AFFECT BUYING HABITS.

Forget the old adage, "Don't believe everything you read." No one believes it. People *do* believe what they read, especially regarding antiques and collectibles.

Trade publications such as *AntiqueWeek, Maine Antique Digest,* and *The Magazine Antiques* are great resources because they concentrate solely on antiques and collectibles. These types of publications impact the market by generating interest in general categories of antiques, such as musical instruments, as well as specific items, like Gibson guitars. The increased exposure and related excitement are usually followed by greater demand.

While these publications are helpful in identifying trends, they can also indicate when a collecting craze has run its course. Two articles on vintage doll houses might denote the beginning of a collecting trend, but eight articles on the same subject might signal that interest is peaking and the craze is about to decline.

Trade publications also serve as a yardstick to measure the market. Auction reports and show reports are helpful in determining where consumer interest is focused. If duck decoys are selling for record amounts or if prices for Arts & Crafts furniture have leveled off, you should adjust your inventory and displays accordingly.

These reports also identify what's hot and what's not and reveal where the market is strong or weak. Use this information to increase your profits. Michigan might be the place to buy Victorian furniture if show reports always list reasonable prices for those items. Or, auction reports might reveal that New York is the best place to sell the vintage clothing gathering dust in your shop in Texas. Sell where the market is strong; buy where the market is weak. Use trade publications as road maps to point you in the right direction.

Advertisements also provide clues to the market. Pay attention to what items collectors are looking for and dealers are promoting. You might learn that several collectors are seeking decorated candle boxes. If you have slide-lid boxes in your inventory, create a display. If dealers who advertise are emphasizing cast-iron lawn furniture, you might try spotlighting those goods.

Pay attention to the advertising campaigns waged by both dealers and collectors. Even the size of the ad can indicate where the market is strong. Three full-page ads for weather vanes might indicate greater demand for these items than do three small ads for Civil War tintypes.

> **FYI**
>
> Examples of publications providing useful information about the market:
>
> - General trade publications
>   - *AntiqueWeek*
>   - *The Magazine Antiques*
>   - *Maine Antique Digest*
> - Specialty trade publications
>   - *Collector Editions*
>   - *Antique Toy World*
>   - *Victoria*
> - Women's magazines
>   - *Better Homes & Gardens*
>   - *Redbook*
> - Decorator magazines
>   - *Home*
>   - *House & Garden*
>   - *House Beautiful*
> - Country magazines
>   - *Country Home*
>   - *Country Living*

Don't overlook the classifieds. They also reveal trends. One ad for early video games might not nudge you away from your morning coffee, but four want ads for Atari's Pong should make you take notice.

Although trade publications are an excellent source of information, don't overlook the influence of general-interest magazines. Readers often want to mimic the looks presented in decorator, country, and women's magazines. Watch for new trends and adjust your inventory accordingly. If a crisper image is replacing the rustic look in kitchen decor, it may be time to change your display. You might find that brightly colored kitchenware of the 1950s sells better than your selection of yellowware.

Pay attention not only to the furniture and accessories highlighted in these magazines, but also to the color schemes and patterns. If a checkered look is the latest fad, promote your gingham tablecloths and your 19th-century game board.

Even newspapers can provide clues to the market. If *USA Today* runs an article on Czechoslovakian dinnerware, interest is bound to rise. Likewise, stories discussing Goofy's 60th birthday or the 80th anniversary of the sinking of the Titanic renew interest in related items.

One word of caution, however: beware media hype that can throw a collecting trend out of control. Cookie jars brought phenomenal prices at the Andy Warhol sale in 1989. When those prices were reported by the media, the market went wild and prices skyrocketed. Ordinary jars brought outrageous prices. For dealers with cookie jars to sell, the media attention was a boon. They were able to sell jars that had gone unnoticed for months. However, some dealers who purchased cookie jars during this craze were stuck with overpriced merchandise when the market leveled off.

7 Follow the Book Market and Other Mass Media

THE ENTERTAINMENT INDUSTRY IS YOUR FRIEND.

Walk into any book store and locate the section reserved for antiques and collectibles. If you can elbow your way past the people browsing there, you'll find shelves of books jumbled together, many copies dog-eared from use. Not the sort of thing you'll see in the etiquette section or the classics.

Extremely popular with collectors and dealers, books dealing with antiques and collectibles wield considerable influence over the market. Everyone, it seems, wants to look through the latest book on American furniture or Depression glass or post-war toys. Because they are so popular, these books can serve as a catalyst to generate interest in a particular field, highlighting new categories of collectibles and stimulating established markets. Consider these interests when planning your displays and inventory.

The publication of a specialty price guide, such as Pauline Flick's *Cat Collectibles,* is a sure sign that an item has mass appeal. A display that includes your wooden Felix doorstop, Chessie playing cards, and Royal Copley kitten figurine will attract cat collectors and capitalize on renewed interest generated by the book.

Books dealing with first-time subject matter often indicate a relatively new field of interest. When initially released, *Hake's Guide to TV Collectibles* focused attention on memorabilia associated with television shows from the 1950s to the 1980s.

Subsequent editions of a book signal continued demand for the subject matter. In its eighth edition, *Petretti's Coca-Cola Collectibles Price Guide* illustrates how a single collectible can intrigue the public for a prolonged period.

General mass-market books can also spark interest in certain antiques and collectibles. When *Scarlett* was released, it was the perfect opportunity for antiques dealers to highlight *Gone With the Wind* items, from books to movie posters. Books such as *Plausible Denial* and *High Treason* focused attention on the assassination of President Kennedy. While the media was once again examining the issue, dealers highlighted memorabilia relating to the former president, from commemorative plates to newspaper accounts of the assassination.

Movies, television programs, theater productions, and songs can also influence what your customers buy. Hollywood is the strongest of these motivators. Extensive publicity campaigns focus the public's attention on the movies.

Reading is Fundamental

It is to your advantage to know what books will soon be released. This allows you to build inventory before new interest in a field increases prices for those items. If the first-ever book on Maxwell House coffee memorabilia is about to be published, expect and plan for greater demand in that area.

The best source for identifying new books is *Forthcoming Books.* Available in the reference section of most libraries, it lists pertinent information about the books, including subject matter, title, author, publishing house, release date, and price.

It is also beneficial to have your name placed on the mailing list of those book companies specializing in topics related to antiques and collectibles. Some of these companies publish semi-annual catalogs which include new releases and their backlist.

"Holy ticket sales!" Look at how effectively Warner Bros. promoted "Batman" and "Batman Returns." Marketing blitzes included massive advertising campaigns and extensive merchandising of new Batman paraphernalia, from toys to T-shirts. A relatively obscure collectible for some time, Batman memorabilia suddenly flew into the spotlight. Dynamic dealers took advantage of this opportunity to highlight their Batman collectibles.

Other types of media can also influence sales. Note what people are watching, reading, listening to, or following in the news.

Capitalize on the public's interest in popular books and movies. A new film about Robin Hood increased demand for related collectibles. Smart dealers set up a display of Robin Hood memorabilia while the movie is still in the limelight.

Television programs such as "Homefront" and "Happy Days" can focus attention on a particular era, increasing interest in furnishings, accessories, and clothing from that period.

Music can also create interest in an overall theme. The popularity of country and western music brought added interest to the field of country collectibles. Likewise, an individual song can draw attention to a specific topic. Elton John's "Candle in the Wind" did more than pay tribute to Marilyn Monroe. It brought her name back to the forefront in the minds of collectors.

Also be aware of current events. Some influences may be obvious. Presidential campaigns always renew interest in political memorabilia. Other headlines will affect the market in a more subtle way. The fall of Communism and the opening of borders in Eastern Europe may result in new markets for antiques and collectibles.

III The Display

There are no simple formulas for creating successful displays. And the mere act of simply displaying goods will not necessarily achieve any valuable result.

Display is primarily a form of direct advertising. It is essentially a practical business, concerned with the relationship between the things to be shown and the people who will be looking at them. To be effective, you must determine the function, goal, and intended target of the display. Lighting, arrangement, and color are then relied upon to achieve the desired effect.

Each browser is an actual or potential customer complete with statistical possibilities of consumption. Your goal is to create displays that attract his attention. Get him to look at your merchandise. The value of advertising via the media is great, but being able to say, "Here is the real thing—come and look," is as great as ever.

Merchandise can sell itself, but it must be effectively showcased in order to do so. Individual items within the display must be coordinated so that they create a harmonious effect which will promote sales. When properly constructed, the overall display will attract potential customers and encourage them to purchase one or more items.

8 Ensure Accessibility and Visibility

THEY WANT IT AND THEY WANT IT NOW!

It's the same story, wherever you go. You're in line at the McDonald's drive-through, just wanting to grab a Big Mac and get back on the road. You might as well be on a Los Angeles freeway at rush hour. No doubt, the occupants of every vehicle in front of you have ordered sandwiches without pickles or fries without salt. You'd swear you could have raised the beef, butchered the cow, and cooked the burger faster than it will take to reach the window.

By the time you get your sandwich, you need aspirin for the migraine you developed while waiting. You stop at the local supermarket. Sure enough, same story. There you are, one tiny bottle of aspirin in your hand. The checkout line in front of you resembles the Continental Divide, carts heaped with mountains of groceries. To make matters worse, the flustered cashier is wearing a badge that pleads, "Please be patient, I'm new." It's enough to make a grown man cry.

The United States has become a nation consumed with the idea of time management. Customers want things quickly and easily. This is true whether they're in the market for a hamburger or a highboy. When those impatient consumers walk into your shop or booth, you'd better be ready for them.

Customers will rapidly scan your merchandise to see if there is anything that piques their interest, deciding in a few seconds whether to take a closer look. When an item merits further examination, it had better be accessible. If not, you are likely to lose the sale. This is particularly true in antique malls, where the dealer is not always present.

A customer may be interested in a double-eagle flask at the back of a high shelf, but he won't attempt to look at it if he can't get it down without

> **▶ FYI**
>
> Ways to create accessibility and visibility:
>
> 1. Put small items in front, large items toward the back.
> 2. Don't bury items. Don't over-stack.
> 3. Provide a step stool if an item is out of reach.
> 4. Don't cram too much into one display. Customers may be reluctant to touch or move that merchandise.

knocking over the cobalt bottles around it. Other shoppers will not pick up an item if they don't think they can return it to its original spot when they are finished.

Avoid these pitfalls by not crowding your shelves with merchandise. Keep a cushion of space between items. A customer will be more likely to examine your flask when he knows he can safely remove it from the display. If that bottle is on an upper shelf that is difficult to reach, provide a step stool.

The customer expects to be serviced in exchange for his money. It is bothersome for a potential customer to locate a mall employee who can unlock a case containing an Eisenberg brooch or who can determine the price of a Royal Bayreuth coachman pitcher on a high shelf. Do your best to minimize the amount of work a customer must do. This may be as simple as letting your shopper know where to go to get a case unlocked or making sure all your merchandise is clearly priced.

Your chances of making a sale increase dramatically when the customer has access to and can handle your merchandise. He generally won't buy

LEFT: You can stifle sales by overwhelming your customers with merchandise. A more-is-better approach actually discourages sales because items are difficult to see and reach. RIGHT: Promote visibility and accessibility by removing some of the clutter and rearranging the merchandise. All the items in this cupboard can be seen and easily removed for inspection.

How Low Can You Go?

Remember that low items are not only difficult to see, but they are also difficult to reach. Two women browsing at an antiques mall emphasized this point. One asked the other, "Is that a piece of Depression glass down there?" Neither one could bend low enough to retrieve the item or even to see it clearly. And the question wasn't important enough to warrant asking an employee to help them.

More accessible placement of the item might have resulted in a sale. Displaying the platter on a dining table or with a shelf of glassware would have provided visibility and accessibility.

what he can't inspect. Once your Niloak Mission Ware candlesticks are in his hands rather than on a shelf, he is more likely to consider purchasing them.

Accessibility has a brother named *visibility*. Your customer won't examine what he can't see.

The importance of visibility is often overlooked when merchandising items on top and bottom shelves. Keep in mind that not every customer is your height. Put yourself on their level. How do things look? Can you see the Adams Rose plates on the top shelf of your corner cupboard, or is a gooseneck teakettle hiding them? Are your Beatrix Potter books visible on the bottom of a bookcase, or are they obscured by shadows?

Additionally, items with labels or obvious fronts lose their impact when they cannot be seen head-on. Your Planters salted peanuts tin won't have an impact if the container is placed too high or low for the customer to see the graphic or if the design is facing the wall. Make frequent checks of your

Don't Become Part of the Problem

Avoid placing yourself between the customer and the merchandise. This happened to us twice during one day.

The first time, a dealer watching television sat in front of a shelving unit full of glassware. She blocked the only aisle leading to that merchandise.

Later in the day, a cashier was reading a magazine behind a showcase at the checkout counter. The magazine was on top of the showcase, concealing the jewelry below. When we looked in the case, she simply slid the magazine from one corner to another. She was not concerned with providing a clear view of the merchandise or allowing us personal space.

The actions of both dealers suggested that we were not legitimate customers and that our business was not important.

display areas and reposition items as necessary. A customer may inadvertently replace your Planters tin upside-down on the shelf; it's up to you to return it to its proper place.

Understand that accessibility and visibility relate to more than just your merchandise. Individuals working in your shop or mall need to be available when customers require assistance. The Illinois Antique Center, a 150-dealer mall in Peoria, Illinois, has implemented this concept extremely well. As many as three employees constantly walk the floors, offering to answer questions, open cases, and carry purchases to the checkout counter. These employees are readily identifiable from their maroon aprons printed with the mall's logo.

9 Create Dimensionality

EVERY DISPLAY HAS ITS UPS AND DOWNS.

Funny thing about skylines. They aren't dramatic if all the buildings are the same height. Add a few skyscrapers, and you've got visual excitement.

The same holds true for displays. Merchandise placed on more than one plane commands attention. And that which is noticed is more likely to sell.

You can create dimensional displays by using risers and easels. Provide variation. Keep the skyline image in mind. Stagger merchandise so that items are not all the same height. Three one-gallon redware storage jars displayed side-by-side don't stand out the way they would if arranged in a stair-stepped manner. When you place those jars at different heights, using boxes or small crates of varying size, the customer's eyes no longer pass quickly over the merchandise. Instead, they travel a varied course through the entire display, focusing on individual items rather than just the exhibit as a whole.

Small items are not the only types of merchandise you should display on different levels. Furniture can also be staggered. Placing your tall-back bed between a chest of drawers and a princess dresser takes advantage of the varied heights of the individual pieces. The dimensionality adds impact to the display.

It is imperative that potential buyers feel comfortable handling the merchandise. When using props such as risers and easels, be sure that they are large enough and stable enough to support the merchandise. You don't want your 9-inch Leeds peafowl plate to tip over because it is supported by an undersized plate holder. Nor do you want your cut glass candy dish to fall off a wobbly riser when the shelf is bumped.

Be innovative. Plate holders and display stands can be used to support more than just plates. Books, photographs, and small stuffed animals can also be displayed in these types of props.

Your own merchandise can also double as risers. Boxes, crates, shelves, and cupboards can be used to hold smaller items. Take care not to overload them, however. You will have a hard time selling your Campbell's Soup crate if it is buried beneath other inventory.

This is also true of furniture your customers might want to thoroughly inspect. At one mall, a customer interested in four cupboards wanted to examine every side of each piece, including the tops and the bottoms. The time-consuming process of unloading and reloading the merchandise displayed in all four cupboards aggravated the shopper and created considerable work for the mall manager.

Use a riser to highlight merchandise. These advertising tins are arranged in the same order in each photo. Without the riser, not every piece can be plainly seen. With the riser, they are all clearly visible.

Floored by a New Idea

Risers that don't rise? That's the idea behind one unique method of highlighting small furniture. A piece of plain linoleum or painted plywood can be used to emphasize your Hepplewhite one-drawer stand or your child's tilt-top table. White usually works best since it contrasts with the color of the furniture and causes the entire ensemble to stand out against almost any floor. Used sparingly, the technique focuses attention on special pieces.

A white board placed under this ten-gallon salt-glazed crock draws attention to the piece by setting it apart from the surrounding merchandise.

10 Use Room Settings

GIVE NEW MEANING TO THE PHRASE "HOME SHOPPING."

Want to attract attention? Redecorate your house. Slide your sofa into the kitchen. Good. Heave your refrigerator into the family room. That's nice. Next, lug your dining room table onto the front porch. Great. Now, shove your bookcase from the den into the bathroom. Excellent. Finally, wheel your lawn mower into the bedroom. Perfect!

Sound crazy? Of course it is. The refrigerator belongs in the kitchen and the sofa should be in the living room. People expect these items to be located in specific places.

Why, then, do so many antiques dealers arrange their merchandise using the bookcase-in-the-bathroom method of decorating? They'll put a boudoir lamp on a kitchen table and a stack of Blue Ridge dishes on a cherry nightstand, never thinking it would make more sense to display them in the opposite manner. Many never even consider arranging their merchandise to create room settings.

Room settings serve as one of the most effective display techniques you can use. Arranging your merchandise in room settings helps your customers to envision those items in their own homes. You become a problem solver instead of just a merchant. For instance, a customer might want to add something to his living room, but he just isn't sure what he is looking for. A turn-of-the-century parlor setting may capture his attention, convincing him that your winged-back chair will be a perfect companion for his marble-top lamp table.

If your shop is in a house, you have a distinct advantage when it comes to creating room settings. You already have the rooms; all you need to do is add the merchandise. There's no question where to put your bathroom scales or your Hoosier cabinet.

▶ FYI

Suggestions for room settings:

1. Living room
2. Dining room
3. Parlor
4. Den or office
5. Bedroom—adult or child
6. Nursery
7. Kitchen
8. Bathroom
9. Entryway
10. Patio, deck, or porch

Room settings help customers picture the merchandise in their own homes. Make your display look natural. Pay attention to details. Here, a lamp, cup and saucer, vintage child's photo, and poetry books accent a lamp table.

However, most shops and malls don't provide a homelike environment, and creating room settings becomes more of a challenge. Antique malls and shows simply offer you an open space, so many feet by so many feet, within which you must work. Because of the space limitations, you may have to create only partial room settings with no walls to define where one display ends and another begins. The only separation between your living room and your kitchen may be a pathway between the two.

11 Include Show-Stoppers

YOU HAVE LESS THAN 15 SECONDS.

Fishermen know the trick. Dangle the right bait and the fish will bite. Put an empty hook in the water and you'll do little more than work on your tan.

The right bait for your customers is anything that sparks their interest. You need an eye-catcher. Actually, you need more than one. Use one show-stopper to grab their attention and encourage them to walk down the aisle to see your booth. Use another to convince them to stop in front of your display. Use a third show-stopper to draw them into your booth. An Illions carousel horse will catch their eye from across the room, a colorful whirligig will make them stop in front of your booth, and an intricate needlepoint sampler will draw them into your display area.

Every buyer was first a looker. Getting shoppers to notice your merchandise is a tough task when the mall or show they are at offers plenty of other items. Attracting the attention of those customers may be difficult, but it's not impossible.

Remember, first impressions are important. Studies show that buyers spend no more than 10 to 15 seconds sizing up an exhibit. Do what you can to ensure they spend more time than that with yours. Convince them to stop and look at your merchandise. Special pieces strategically displayed in highly visible locations can generate interest, prolonging the amount of time the customer spends in your booth and increasing your chance of making a sale.

Where do you locate your show-stoppers? That's easy enough to determine. Look at your booth from a distance—from across the room or down

What's a Show-Stopper?

A show-stopper is any interesting or unusual item that you place in a highly visible location to attract customers.

Neon signs have typically been used by traditional retailers to generate consumer interest. Bold and bright both day and night, they always stand out.

An exquisite cut glass table lamp or delicately proportioned Queen Ann highboy can achieve the same effect. Any spectacular piece can serve as an eye-catcher.

Pay particular attention to colors. The eye tends to gravitate toward vivid colors. Your black-and-purple Amish quilt displayed on the back wall of your booth will be noticed from a distance. Likewise, your bright-yellow Bakelite Fada radio will stand out on almost any shelf.

Show-stoppers are effective tools for attracting customers. Adding five eye-catching items gives this booth a new appearance, even though none of the original merchandise was moved.

Show-Stoppers II: The Sequel

Show-stoppers can also be used to direct your customer to various parts of your booth. By placing high-interest items in each showcase, display, and room setting, you effectively lead the customer from one section of your booth to another. Their prolonged attention increases your chances of making a sale.

the aisle. The spot your eye lands on first is where your initial show-stopper should be placed. Next, stand in front of your booth and look in. Again, the spot your eye focuses on first is where another show-stopper is needed.

When placing show-stoppers, keep in mind that customers may come toward your booth from more than one direction. Maximize the impact of key items by locating them where they are visible from as many angles as possible.

Once you have added show-stoppers to your booth, stand back and take a long objective look. Is anything missing? Are there parts of your display that seem lackluster? If so, pick a dominant item from your inventory and add it to that spot. As only one of many booths at a mall or show, is your display prominent or is it inconspicuous? The creative use of show-stoppers will make your booth a standout.

12 Offer Impulse Items

GOTTA BUY IT!

"68-Year-Old Woman Gives Birth to Two-Headed Alien!" screams the headline as you place your loaf of bread and gallon of milk on the supermarket conveyor belt. All of a sudden it seems vitally important that you find out more about this amazing woman and the extraordinary alien.

Why are tabloids located at supermarket checkout lanes? Because they are impulse items. You didn't go to the store intending to buy that newspaper, yet you couldn't help but scan the front page as you waited in line. You paid the ninety-five cents because something caught your eye or tickled your fancy.

Like traditional retailers, antiques dealers can use impulse items to increase sales. Trade papers, refinishing supplies, and replacement hardware are examples of goods your customers may want or need, but which they might not have considered when they were shopping.

What's an Impulse Item?

Checkout lines are full of impulse items—everything from magazines to candy bars, flashlight batteries to toenail clippers. We've all made these unplanned purchases. The car floor mats were on your shopping list; the tire gauge hanging at the cash register was a last-minute addition.

Promote impulse items with attractive displays. Use a shelf-talker to add emphasis or further explain the product or merchandise. The shelf-talker and display work together to encourage shoppers to try this multi-purpose polish.

FYI

Antiques-related impulse items:

1. Trade papers
2. Shop guides
3. Reference books
4. Trade/decorator magazines
5. Wax, oil, and cleaning supplies
6. Refinishing supplies
7. Replacement hardware
8. Caning supplies
9. Hats and T-shirts with mall logos
10. Inventory books and software

Generally, these items should be located in an area separate from your antiques and collectibles. Although it is acceptable to incorporate a few jars of silver cleaner into your display of sterling flatware, most impulse items should be displayed near the checkout counter. This is your last chance to show your customer those items he might not have initially considered purchasing.

Properly displayed, even your antiques and collectibles become impulse items. Flowers in vases and candles in candlesticks show your customer that your merchandise has an immediate use. He may not have originally intended to buy a piece of pottery, but the floral sprig in your Muncie vase reminds him he needs something to hold the tiger lilies growing in his back yard.

13 Maintain Paths and Personal Space

UNCOMFORTABLE CUSTOMERS ARE STINGY WITH THEIR TIME AND MONEY.

Some booths are nothing more than an obstacle course. You need hiking boots and knee pads just to get through them. If you aren't squeezing between a dresser and a washstand, you're stepping over a doll cradle and a box of dishes.

A clear and definite path is a necessary feature of every display area. Guide customers through your booth with aisles that provide ample room for movement and permit easy access to the merchandise.

Although this technique should be used by all antiques and collectibles dealers, it is of particular importance for show dealers. Large crowds and limited space are special circumstances these dealers must consider when setting up their booths.

Several key factors will determine the location of paths through your booth. One element to consider when designing your layout is the location of your cash drawer. The checkout area should be easily accessible and clearly visible. It should have enough space around it that nearby merchandise is not blocked when several customers are waiting in line.

Pay particular attention to the arrangement of your display tables. Be sure there are no protruding corners customers might bump into. Think of the "Ouch!" factor. Hurt or unhappy customers seldom make purchases.

Some types of merchandise require more space than others. This is particularly true for smalls such as postcards and jewelry. Because customers spend more time looking at these items, you should place this merchandise in an area that does not obstruct the view of the booth or block a pathway.

It doesn't matter from which direction your customers come and go.

Tell Them Where to Go

At times it will be necessary to provide additional information regarding your shop or mall. Use signs to tell shoppers that more antiques are located upstairs or that an outbuilding contains furniture in the rough. Rooms that are off limits to the public should also be clearly marked. A simple but courteous sign such as "Employees only" removes any confusion your shoppers might have.

What is important, however, is that you show them where to go by providing a clear path connecting the entrance and the exit. Two entrance/exit areas avoid the bottlenecks caused when all your customers come and go from the same point. This is especially true at shows and flea markets,

A clear path enables customers to easily access all the merchandise in a booth. These photos picture the same items. The difference between a cluttered mess and an orderly display is obvious.

▶ FYI

Special considerations for show dealers:

1 Cash box: Place the cash box in an easily accessible location that will not block traffic.

2 Display cases: Put display cases where there is ample room in front for the customer to examine the merchandise. Leave yourself enough space to open the case and access its contents.

3 Postcards, books, etc.: Provide extra space so that customers feel comfortable spending additional time looking through this merchandise. Locate the display so that browsers will not obstruct another section of your booth.

4 Entrances and exits: Avoid bottlenecks caused when people must enter and exit at the same point. Having two or more entrance/exits prevents this problem.

5 Traffic flow: Remember, shows can generate a high volume of traffic in a short period of time. Plan your booth accordingly. Use wide aisles and provide additional space in front of displays.

where large numbers of people pass through your booth in a short amount of time.

Although pathways are important, equal attention should be devoted to preserving each customer's personal space. Keeping booths open and uncluttered gives your buyers the chance to ease themselves into their surroundings. A booth that seems too crowded or too small thrusts the buyer and the seller into each other's personal space. A customer who is uncomfortable because of this will not spend any more time than necessary in your booth.

Encroaching too quickly or too aggressively on the shopper's personal space can kill a sale. Although customers like to know assistance is available when needed, they don't want the dealer to follow them from room to room or badger them with questions.

14 Group Items by Theme

GO WITH THE GO-WITHS.

Traditional retailers have long used themes to sell their merchandise. A local drugstore recently put a brand of bubble bath on sale. Instead of merely placing a "SALE" banner on the appropriate shelf, the employees filled a claw-footed bathtub with the product and added a catchy sign to emphasize the sale. What a great idea.

Antiques dealers can use the same approach. There's no need to have Kentucky Derby glasses on a shelf, race programs in a showcase, and a print of Secretariat on the wall. Maximize their impact by putting them all in one eye-catching display. Or, group animal-related advertising tins on a wooden Lion Coffee crate. A shelf-talker outlining the historical significance of animals in advertising will tie everything together.

Grouping items according to theme can encourage the sale of go-withs. Displaying vintage photographs with cameras and photo-related advertising can induce a collector in one field to purchase an item from a related field. A camera collector might be on the lookout for Kodak signs, but he may not know that some vintage Hallmark cards have a camera motif.

Using an era theme is another possibility. Highlight merchandise from a specific time period. The display could show a typical living room from the 1940s, vintage clothing from the 1920s, or children's toys from the turn of the century.

Use shelf-talkers to emphasize your thematic displays. These brief informational signs can be used to unify a display and educate the consumer. They are especially helpful when particular pieces are unfamiliar to the customer.

Holidays are ideal times for setting up thematic displays. Valentine's Day, Easter, and Christmas are three holidays used by traditional retailers to promote sales. Other holidays might not warrant the strong sales approach, but they can still be used as the focus of a thematic display. Your Independence Day display doesn't have to be the traditional red, white, and blue. It can incorporate a variety of patriotic items, including a World War II navy uniform, an *American Legion Magazine*, and a Statue of Liberty figurine.

Ideas for creating thematic displays can come from a number of sources. Start with the obvious. Most calendars list holidays and major events.

Chase's Annual Events provides an interesting and thorough list of celebrations and anniversaries. The book covers more than just typical

Use a theme approach to combine unrelated categories of antiques and collectibles in one unified display. This sports display incorporates clothing, advertising, vintage photos, athletic equipment, and pyrography.

holidays. It also outlines obscure celebrations such as National Zoo & Aquarium Month and National Clock Month. *Chase's* can be found in the reference section of your local library and in some bookstores.

Gift shops are ideal places for borrowing ideas because the merchandise often promotes holidays and special events. A card for a golden wedding anniversary or wrapping paper for a baby shower might prompt you to build displays around those themes.

▶ FYI

Holidays and celebrations to consider for thematic displays:

- Valentine's Day
- Presidents' Day
- St. Patrick's Day
- Easter
- Mother's Day
- Armed Forces Day
- Memorial Day
- Flag Day
- Father's Day
- Independence Day
- Columbus Day
- Halloween
- Election Day
- Veterans Day
- Thanksgiving
- Hanukkah and Christmas

15 Group Items by Color or Pattern

USE COLOR TO PUT YOURSELF IN THE BLACK.

Time for a quick round of multiple-choice Jeopardy! We supply the answer, you pick the correct question. Good luck.

The answer is: Kitchens and Bathrooms.

Which is the correct question?

a In which two rooms of the house is water most commonly used?

b What is the title of a Time/Life how-to book on home repair?

c Which two rooms are most often decorated according to a color scheme?

The correct response is "c." (Okay, all three are correct, but it's our book, and we pick "c.") Color is often the main consideration when decorating kitchens and bathrooms. A kitchen may be accessorized with red-and-white checkered curtains, a bright-red canister set, and red-handled utensils. A bathroom might be decorated with an Atkinson Fox garden

When grouped together, patterned items can grab the customer's attention. One Blue Willow plate might be overlooked, but eight pieces in a display will turn a few heads.

Treeing a Related Idea

The idea of using color to create displays also works well with furniture.

Some people like light woods such as pine, maple, and oak. Others prefer dark woods such as walnut, cherry, and mahogany. You can capitalize on this preference by grouping furniture according to color or type of wood. Place your Mission oak Morris chair with a maple end table, or put a cherry nightstand next to your walnut spool bed.

print, a green glass towel rod, and a green transferware pitcher and bowl set.

Why is this color business so important? Because understanding what shoppers are looking for when they walk into your booth helps you to present merchandise in ways that will appeal to them.

Many people decorate according to color, and they may be inclined to purchase a particular item simply because it matches the decor. A single item can attract attention solely because of its color; a group of items of the same color can create a powerful visual image that is difficult to ignore. Take advantage of color's impact to create displays that will attract shoppers and encourage sales.

Remember to rotate items out of these areas occasionally so that customers not interested in a particular color do not ignore the display and miss something they would normally have purchased for a different reason. Someone searching for covered animal dishes might miss your brown hen-on-nest because they passed by your display of chocolate glass.

Your display does not have to be limited to items from just one category of collectibles, such as glassware. Be creative. Display together any items that are related. For a red kitchen display, you might include dishes, glasses, red-handled utensils, mixing bowls, canister sets, napkins, towels, aprons, advertising tins and bottles, and red-trimmed graniteware.

In addition to color, you can also group items according to pattern. Autumn Leaf items are an excellent choice for creating a patterned display. Your display need not focus solely on dinnerware. Incorporate other merchandise that also carries the Jewel Tea motif. This might include a tablecloth, a wastebasket, a cake holder, shelf paper, and a deck of playing cards.

16 Group Items by Price

THE PRICE IS RIGHT.

One of the latest trends in retail malls is the $1 store. Everything in the store is priced at a buck. No more. No less. People love the idea. They walk through the door expecting to find a bargain.

You can also display your antiques and collectibles according to price. Two methods are most commonly used: grouping items by a single price and grouping them within a price range.

The single-price method works like the dollar stores. All items on a particular shelf are $5, or each piece on a certain table is $25.

The second method incorporates items having prices within a specific range. All items in a designated display are less than $10, or all items are priced between $20 and $50.

These types of displays work because they hook the bargain hunters as well as those people on a limited budget. It is senseless for your customer to be looking at $100 crystal wine glasses when he only has $20 in his wallet, but you can still catch his attention with your display of $10 glassware. When he sees your set of pressed glass beer steins he might decide, "It doesn't get any better than this."

Make sure each item displayed has its own price tag. If someone moves a $600 Shirley Temple doll to your table of $25 merchandise, you want the customer to immediately realize that it doesn't belong there.

Remember, using prices to define your displays will only work when your patrons understand the concept. Use signs to ensure customers know that everything on the front table is priced under $50.

Every Day's a Holiday

Grouping items by price is especially effective in promoting merchandise as gifts.

People are always shopping for gifts, and they are generally working within a budget. Grouping a number of same-price items together decreases the amount of time your customer must spend searching for merchandise he can afford. If he only has $25 to spend, he might just glance at your booth and move on. However, a sign promoting items "$25 or Less" will draw him to your table of specially priced merchandise. The display can contain items as diverse as corkscrews and first-edition books. What's of primary importance to your customer is the possibility of finding a gift in his price range.

Customers on a budget will appreciate this selection of merchandise grouped by price. A shelf-talker which reads "All items on this table are $25 or less" promotes this display.

Keep in mind that consumers often associate price with quality. You can prevent the notion that these pieces are cheap or somehow inferior by periodically rotating items out of these special displays.

17 Show the Original Use

IT'S TIME TO BE DEMONSTRATIVE.

Tire kickers. Browsers. Sunday shoppers.

Call them what you want. The name doesn't really matter. They are what they are—people who meander into your shop or booth without intending to buy anything. They're just killing time or spending a pleasant afternoon window shopping.

Some dealers hate them, cursing under their breath when yet another person holds up a relic from his childhood and says with pride, "I used to have one of these, but I threw it away."

Seldom are these customers big spenders. The purchases they make are usually inexpensive. After all, they aren't there to buy. They're there to look.

Tire kickers. Browsers. Sunday shoppers. Who needs 'em?

You do.

If you're bothered by such individuals, you've got the wrong attitude. These are the very customers you need to be targeting because they don't necessarily plan to spend any money. When an effective display convinces them that a particular antique or collectible will look good in their home, Bingo! You've made a sale you wouldn't have made otherwise.

The key to producing these types of sales is to understand your customer. A number of shoppers aren't concerned with an item's value as a collectible. They simply know what they like. If they are interested in your Van Briggle vase, it is because it's blue, because it matches their dining room, or because you displayed it well. They couldn't care less that it's a piece of hand-thrown art pottery.

How do you sell to someone who isn't necessarily interested in buying? By displaying an item as it was originally intended to be used, you can help

> **FYI**
>
> Items which can be displayed together to demonstrate original use:
>
> 1. Toothpicks in a toothpick holder
> 2. Dishes in a wire drainer
> 3. Sacks in a sack holder
> 4. Checkers on a checkerboard
> 5. Doilies under lamps and vases
> 6. Napkins in napkin rings
> 7. Knives on knife rests
> 8. Crackers in a cracker jar
> 9. Letters in a letter holder
> 10. Coats on a coat rack

Showing an item's intended use helps the customer visualize it in his own home. These dishes and accessories look unimpressive until arranged in a table setting. Candles and flowers complete the look.

that customer to visualize the item in his own home. Set a table rather than leave it bare, put candles in candlesticks, and place spoons in a spooner. Your blue Roseville Pinecone vase can sell itself. However, you can emphasize its functional aspects by filling it with flowers and using it as the centerpiece for a round oak table.

Likewise, an empty Lance peanuts jar is a missed opportunity. Buy some whole peanuts and put them in the jar. Now it's functional as well as decorative. Some peanut-loving customer is bound to notice. He might not be looking for a peanut jar, but he also might not be able to resist yours once he sees it.

When showing original use, you should also demonstrate that the item works. When was the last time you walked into a lighting store that had all the lamps turned off? Let the customer know that your Tiffany floor lamp works, and that it provides a warm, inviting glow. If you display your lamp without a light bulb and with the cord wrapped around the base, it is extremely difficult for him to appreciate its charm.

18 Show New Uses

AND NOW FOR SOMETHING COMPLETELY DIFFERENT.

Christopher Columbus is sitting in an open-air cafe in Spain, talking to a couple of royal businessmen in three-piece suits.

"It's guaranteed to work," Chris says. "I sail west to get to the East."

"Go west to get east? I don't know. The King's pretty iffy about this one," the First Suit says. "Go over that again. How's that possible?"

"Simple. If I sail west far enough, west becomes east. And, what's in the east? The *East* Indies. All I need is a little support—some upfront money, some men, and five ships."

"We still don't know, Chris," the Second Suit remarks. "It sounds awfully crazy. Word of this plan of yours has gotten around, and people are beginning to talk. They're saying you conked your head on a mast one too many times. What if you're wrong? The King just doesn't need that kind of embarrassment."

Turn the ordinary into the extraordinary. Show innovative uses for items. This Ful-O-Pep pamphlet holder appropriately displays a runner's race numbers and medallions.

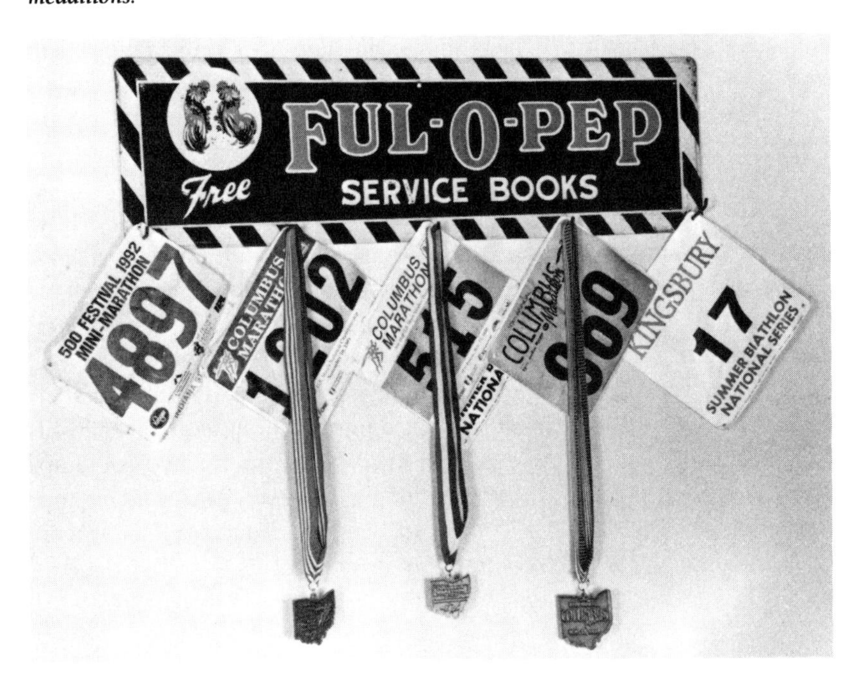

▶ FYI

Antiques and collectibles used in a non-traditional manner:

1. Redware bowl containing gold Christmas balls
2. Small wicker basket storing rolls of toilet paper
3. Blue-decorated crock serving as a recycling bin
4. Cast-iron grate hanging as artwork
5. Oak wardrobe functioning as an entertainment center

"Okay. Okay. Four ships and I'm happy. That should lessen the royal burden."

"We're taking a big chance with this one, Chris," the First Suit responds. "A big chance. What's your stake in this? What've you got to lose? Your life? Pfffff. We're talking about face for the First Family."

"There has to be a trade-off?" Chris asks, fidgeting with his cup of cappuccino.

"Okay," the Second Suit says. "Call us crazy. Three ships, and it's a deal."

"Deal!" Chris exclaims.

The rest, as they say, is history.

Okay, so it didn't work out quite like Columbus planned. He was prevented from sailing to the East Indies when the Americas got in his way. The important point is that he wasn't afraid to implement a new idea, to try something different.

You, too, can demonstrate a little of Columbus's creativity by showing customers innovative, non-traditional uses for some of the antiques and collectibles you sell. It won't get you a New World, but it might improve

When You Can't Think of it Yourself

You can borrow ideas for new-use displays from a number of sources.

Magazines such as *Country Living* and *Victoria* are great for showing innovative uses for items. Though the text may be interesting, it is the photographs which are particularly helpful in this case.

Never underestimate the influence of a friend. Don't be afraid to imitate their creative ideas.

Don't forget to capitalize on the resourcefulness of other dealers. Their displays might be worth copying.

your sales. Try showcasing your Hall Cattail dinnerware on a baker's pie rack or use a graniteware angel food cake pan to store kitchen towels. Such approaches can help sell otherwise ordinary items.

One dealer at an October flea market even found a new use for a glass chicken waterer. Filled with candy corn, the jar became a colorful Halloween item. His creativity turned an otherwise nondescript item into a decorative and useful collectible.

A variation on the new-use theme is to mix and match china. Varied place settings are the rage. A customer may not want six complete place settings of your Noritake Azalea, but the bread plates look great with the Lenox dinner plates they are considering buying.

You can also mix and match your glassware. Display crystal with colored glass. Royal Ruby and clear glassware is a particularly stunning combination.

19 Offer New Types of Merchandise

STAGNATION STINKS. CLEAR THE AIR.

We are creatures of habit. We know what we like, and we tend not to stray from that course. We are accustomed to watching certain television shows, reading particular types of books, buying specific newspapers, and shopping for a set style of clothing. We find comfort in the familiar.

As a dealer in the antiques and collectibles business, you are no different. You may tend to carry only certain types of merchandise—buying cut glass but avoiding Fiesta ware, purchasing vintage photos but neglecting watercolors. If you specialize in particular items, this is fine. If you sell a general line of merchandise, it can be a costly oversight.

A dealer who carries only dolls will not consider purchasing a collection of World's Fair postcards. This is only logical. But it would be foolish for a general-line dealer in St. Louis, the site of the 1904 World's Fair, not to consider buying them, even if he has never dealt in postcards.

Customers are bored when they find the same types of merchandise in every booth. Varied inventory will attract their attention. A dealer who experiments with his stock might even discover a line that sells especially well. If your antique mall is filled with glassware and furniture, you might incorporate some vintage clothing. Add a few pieces to your existing displays by putting aprons with kitchenware or nightclothes with bedroom furniture.

Be Daring; Swim Upstream

As a dealer, you can capitalize on new fads and trends. An item unnoticed this year might spawn a collectible craze next year. Be flexible. Take a chance. Consider stocking such items *before* they become popular.

With the advent of compact discs, LP albums have become the dinosaurs of today's music industry. As such, a good portion of these albums have been discarded by music lovers. Many sell for next to nothing at flea markets.

Yet, if album covers were to suddenly be considered a type of art form, their desirability might increase. Both the demand for and price of these items would rise.

Don't overlook a new collecting trend. You might be surprised by your ability to predict and anticipate movement within the market.

20 Separate Old from New

ANTIQUES DEMAND A SOLO PERFORMANCE.

Phrases you've heard before:

a The check is in the mail
b I gave at the office
c This will only hurt a little

With so many people saying so many things that simply aren't true, it's hard to know who to believe. Your shoppers have the same problem. They simply want to patronize someone they can trust.

As a dealer, one of your most important assets is your reputation. When customers trust you, they will buy from you. That trust can be quickly lost, though, when they doubt the authenticity of your merchandise.

The best way to gain and keep trust is to limit your merchandise to true antiques and collectibles. Many of your customers are not knowledgeable about your merchandise. All they know is that the sign outside your shop advertises "ANTIQUES" in large bold letters. When they walk through your door, that's what they expect to find. Antiques. Not new items. Not reproductions.

You might know that one of these still banks is an original and the other is a reproduction, but your customer might not be able to tell the difference. Labeling the newer bank as a reproduction prevents confusion and demonstrates your honesty.

One Trick Pony

If the reproduction Victorian rocking horse you bought last week fooled you, it will most certainly trick many of your customers. Use it as an educational tool.

Display the horse with a prominent sign that provides as much information as possible. Emphasize that the item is a reproduction. Supply dates if available. Explain the features that distinguish it from an authentic Victorian rocking horse.

Acknowledging your mistake reinforces your credibility as a reputable dealer. It preserves your integrity at the same time that it creates goodwill. Customers will feel secure about buying your merchandise because they are confident that you do not intend to take advantage of them.

Some dealers argue that clearly labeling items as reproductions is enough. One such dealer displays reproduction signs in his booth and writes "Not Old" on the price tags. Unfortunately, the signs are mixed with his vintage merchandise. They cast doubt on everything he carries. Now the customer wonders about the authenticity of that dealer's Trick Dog mechanical bank. Did the dealer simply forget to identify it as a contemporary piece? Has the tag fallen off and been lost? Is the dealer trying to make a quick buck by passing off a new piece as a reproduction?

If you do decide to sell new items and/or reproductions, isolate that merchandise in a special area: be sure the items are clearly tagged as reproductions. Also, use shelf-talkers to further identify those items and tell why you are carrying them. Explain that you offer reproduction folk art weather vanes because authentic examples are prohibitively expensive and difficult to find.

The antiques and collectibles industry has long hidden behind the phrase *caveat emptor:* Let the buyer beware! Some dealers assume that anyone so uninformed as to be fooled by a reproduction deserves to be stuck with that item.

The trouble with this philosophy is that not everyone who gets stung by a reproduction sees it as a learning experience. Anyone would be bitter if he discovered that the R.S. Prussia bowl he purchased at a major show is a fake.

Angry, unhappy people do not make good customers. More than likely, that individual will never again purchase anything from the dealer who sold him the bowl. Worse yet, it is entirely possible he will stop buying antiques altogether.

Although this scenario might be extreme, it isn't unrealistic. Reproduc-

The Good, the Bad, and the Ugly

Are reproductions always bad? No. Many serve a legitimate purpose. They are affordable copies of vintage items that, because of their rarity, are either unavailable or unaffordable.

Reproductions become a problem when they are presented as authentic antiques by unscrupulous or uninformed dealers. Many customers might not be able to tell whether a wicker doll buggy is an antique worth $400 or a reproduction worth only $100.

Avoid uncertainty and confusion. Separate new items and reproductions from your antiques and collectibles. Clearly label all your merchandise so shoppers understand what's new and what's antique.

tions have tainted the antiques industry. Their proliferation—from cut glass toothpick holders to tiger maple corner cupboards—has made many shoppers wary. Some have even adopted a get-tough stance, refusing to patronize dealers who mix reproductions and new items with their vintage antiques and collectibles.

The solution? Don't mix reproductions and new items with vintage merchandise. It's as simple as that. Finding buyers for your newly made Victorian-style bird cages might not be difficult. But, that short-term profit could be jeopardizing both the integrity and the future of your business.

21 Highlight Fresh Merchandise

WHO WANTS WILTED WARES?

If collecting is an addiction, then fresh merchandise is the drug. Customers love to see items they've not looked at before. Repeatedly offer them merchandise they've never seen, and you've got them hooked. Trips to your booth will become a habit they can't break.

The obsessive search for fresh merchandise is best exemplified at outdoor antique shows where customers are allowed on the grounds while dealers are setting up. Most dealers don't even make it to their space in the field without having interested show-goers walking or running beside the vehicle, looking to see what's for sale, and making offers on the spot. Even more common is the sight of shoppers going through boxes before the dealer can get his merchandise unpacked and displayed.

Fresh merchandise attracts customers. Maximize its magnetic force by placing your new items in a highly-visible area. Show frequent shoppers you are constantly restocking. Give them a reason to walk into your booth and look around.

Placement of fresh merchandise is of paramount importance. Always try to put some of your new merchandise in a highly visible spot at the front of your display area. Remember, the intent is to show frequent customers you make a conscious effort to present items that were not on display the last time they visited. If you're bringing a newly acquired bird's-eye maple chest of drawers into your booth, place it close to the front so it can be readily spotted. Or, highlight your newly purchased Winnie the Pooh game by making it the central item of a children's display.

Like show-stoppers, fresh merchandise can also be placed in highly visible locations at the rear of your displays. Put your eight-foot-tall walnut bookcase and your circus freak show banner at the back of your booth. These items will attract the attention of your customers and draw them into your booth.

In addition to attracting customers to your booth, fresh merchandise encourages shoppers to spend more time examining your displays. A silver buyer may have looked at your display of sterling hollow ware twenty times, but he'll look a little longer the twenty-first time if he sees that you've added fresh stock. Even a Gorham nut dish can hold his attention, providing it is displayed prominently enough to catch his eye. Having spotted the nut dish, he'll take a closer look to see what else you might have added.

Likewise, shoppers who aren't looking for something specific will

Save it for Later

How often you add fresh merchandise to your shop or booth depends, in part, on how often you are able to buy new stock. However, displaying all of your recent finds at once may not be the most effective merchandising technique. Save some items to be added later. This is particularly useful when you know that you will not have an opportunity to buy new merchandise for a prolonged period.

Plan ahead. If you know that a hospital stay will keep you from buying for two weeks, set back some fresh stock in anticipation. When you leave the hospital, you will already have merchandise on hand that can be channelled into your booth.

spend more time in your booth if they know it contains fresh merchandise. Frequent shoppers tend to just glance over those booths that appear unchanged from previous visits. They assume that everything has remained the same. It is your job to convince them this is not so. When you attract their attention with new and exciting merchandise, those shoppers will spend extra time looking for Waldo—searching your booth to discover what has been added.

Displaying fresh merchandise is especially important for show dealers. Whether it's a recurring show or different shows in the same region, customers won't waste their time with merchandise they've seen previously. Show-goers hate to see the same items offered show after show, even if those events are held a year apart. They want to buy merchandise they haven't looked at before. When you give them that opportunity, when you prominently display fresh merchandise, you draw them into your booth and are more likely to make a sale.

22 Remove Stale Merchandise

THROW THE BUMS OUT!

If antiquers love to see fresh merchandise, they hate to see stale merchandise. In some shops or malls, merchandise has been around so long it's practically a landmark. When customers start using it as a point of reference for giving directions, it's been there too long. "Straight past the Buster Brown poster, hang a left at the fifteen-gallon Western crock, and it's right past the Berghoff crate."

You're familiar with the scene. The copper apple butter kettle has been in the same spot in the antique shop for the past four years. The dealer doesn't seem to care if the piece *ever* sells. And, you're so used to seeing it there that you fully expect it to still be gathering dust the next time you visit the shop.

That's not good.

Displays should constantly change. One way to accomplish this is to remove stale merchandise—anything that hasn't sold after a set period of time.

Unfortunately, there's no magical formula for determining when an item has been displayed too long. And, the same time frame should not be applied to all your merchandise. You might feel comfortable leaving your

Know When to No-Show

Merchandise is advertising. It sets the stage for everything that is to follow. While it is important for shop and mall dealers to remove stale merchandise, it is vital that show dealers follow this rule.

Shows attract a large number of infrequent shoppers—people who do not regularly visit antique shops and malls. An individual may see your merchandise only once a year. When he walks into your booth, he had better not find the same items you displayed during the last show. If much of your merchandise hasn't changed, there's little reason for him to spend time looking at your goods. When he sees the Flow Blue pitcher and turn-of-the-century wedding dress you offered at last year's show, you're in trouble. Thinking you don't have *any* fresh merchandise, he hurries to the next booth. You just lost a customer.

Avoid this problem by keeping records of what you take to each show. An inventory sheet listing your merchandise will tell you which Staffordshire historical plates you took to this year's show. When you're planning next year's show, you'll know you should take those historical plates you haven't offered there before.

Tiffany desk lamp on display for more than a year, but you might want to consider removing your Ex-Lax thermometer after only four months.

Stale merchandise presents a negative image to your customers. When they see that you still have your John Deere pedal tractor after two years, they are likely to think it is overpriced, undesirable, or defective. If they do, they'll also assume you aren't a very good dealer. Those shoppers will be less likely to buy from you.

What are your options? First, decide how long you feel comfortable displaying each piece of merchandise. If you just bought a Victorian wrought-iron aquarium stand, develop a game plan before you put the item on display.

You might decide that you want to sell the stand within six months. You bought it at the beginning of January and immediately put it in your shop. Make a note in your inventory that you will remove the piece from the sales floor if it hasn't sold by the end of June. Next, decide how long you will leave the item at its original price before you begin to mark it down. In this

Customers who find stale merchandise in your booth will assume you have nothing worth buying. The cobwebs, dust, and dirty merchandise in this photograph have been exaggerated, but the point is clear. Items that have been displayed for too long suggest the dealer doesn't care about his merchandise or his customers.

Too Much of a Good Thing

Some dealers believe that more is better. They crowd their shops with merchandise, assuming the increased inventory will result in increased sales. Yet, it doesn't always work that way. A potential buyer can be overwhelmed by too much merchandise. Rather than focusing on your cat's-eye pepper pot, he'll only notice the cluttered shelf it's on. Avoid this problem by removing some of the extra merchandise so the pepper pot can be seen readily. Sometimes the less-is-better approach is most effective.

case, you decide that you will put the stand on sale in five months—at the beginning of June—if it hasn't sold.

Once the stand is on the sales floor, your work isn't done. During the first five months, at full price, you should occasionally move it within the display area. Use the piece in several settings. Put it in a living room setting one month, use it as part of a fish display the next month, and place it with other wrought-iron pieces the following month. Each display focuses on a different characteristic of the stand. A person who doesn't collect fish memorabilia might want it as an interesting addition to his collection of wrought-iron furniture.

After five months, put the stand on sale. If the piece still hasn't sold by the end of June—your original target date—remove it from the showroom floor. Put it in storage, sell it at an auction or, if you set up in more than one shop or mall, rotate it to another location.

'Tis No Longer the Season

Holiday items make perfect displays when in season. However, that merchandise becomes stale once the holiday is over.

Unless you sell Christmas items year-round, you will want to take down your Christmas displays by New Year's Day. If your chalkware nativity scene, cast-iron tree stand, and box of Noma bubble lights are still for sale in the middle of January, customers might think that nothing has been changed in your booth for the last month.

Optimally, holiday-related displays should be removed the day after the holiday. That merchandise can still be sold; just don't give it prominent billing as a holiday item. At the end of November, move your glass turkey out of your Thanksgiving display and into your exhibit of candy containers. When you take down your Christmas display in late December, move your Mickey Mouse Christmas lights to a special display of Disney memorabilia.

▶ FYI

Factors that affect your decision to remove merchandise:

1 The item itself—your $600 Shaker sewing basket should be displayed longer than your $6 comic book.

2 Time of year—your wool bathing suit should be displayed during summer months and your hockey skates during the winter.

3 Space considerations—a recently purchased sideboard might displace several smaller pieces of furniture.

4 Economy—your utilitarian floor lamp will sell better during a recession than your decorative John Rogers sculpture.

5 Trends—a Star Trek phaser may beam in and out of popularity with movie and television sequels.

Of course, the best way to remove stale merchandise is to sell it. Many dealers refuse to sell an item for less than their original investment. However, understand that you have capital tied up in each piece. If you've had an item for an extended period of time, be willing to sell it at a loss. Realize that you are in the business to make money. If an item doesn't sell, it's tying up capital. Be willing to get at least a part of your money back so you can stock something more saleable. Accept a loss if that's what it takes to move the item.

Selling an item at a loss isn't always bad. If you offer someone a good deal, he's going to remember you. Customers frequent shops and malls where they have found bargains. They tend to pass by those shops that never seem to have the right merchandise at the right price.

23 Rearrange Often

YOU *CAN* TEACH AN OLD BOOTH NEW TRICKS.

A mall owner confided that he hadn't seen one of his dealers in more than a month and a half. Needless to say, the dealer's booth looked the same then as it had six weeks earlier. The only difference was that no one had straightened during that six-week period. Same merchandise, same displays, bigger mess.

Customers want to see fresh merchandise every time they walk into your shop or booth. However, the basic problem every dealer faces is the quest for new items. To encourage repeat business you must convey the impression that your inventory is exciting, well-priced, and constantly changing.

One way to accomplish this is to keep buying new stock. Unfortunately, this is not a practical solution for most dealers. Not only are antiques both costly and difficult to find, but you also have only so much space to work with.

It is possible to create an impression of freshness without any inventory change. Just keep moving things around. Change your displays at least every few weeks. Move both big and little items, individual pieces and entire displays. Don't just rearrange your display of jigsaw puzzles, move them to another part of your booth. Don't just move your 1950s breakfast table, change the place settings as well.

Though we all look, we do not always "see." It is an interesting phenomenon experienced by every dealer—a customer will come in and

How Much is that Doggie in the Window?

In addition to rearranging merchandise in your booth, you also need to change your window displays.

For the casual passer-by, an item in the window can be the magnet that pulls him into your shop. He might not be interested in antiques and collectibles, but his grandmother had a cast-iron Airedale doorstop just like the one displayed in your window. That dog may catch his attention and bring him into your shop. "Granny had a dog just like that," he'll proudly tell you. "But we threw it into the holler when we tore down the house. I didn't know it was worth *that* much. You don't mind if I look around, do you?" Your window display just created a customer.

Rearranging your merchandise gives frequent customers a reason to look around your booth again. Moving individual pieces or entire displays can stimulate sales by increasing interest in your merchandise. These two photographs show the same corner before and after the booth was rearranged.

Nothing new was added to this booth, yet it looks completely different with the merchandise rearranged. Shoppers accustomed to seeing the dog items, vintage photographs, sporting goods, and stoneware are pleasantly surprised to find those displays replaced by children's items, framed prints, and a simple room setting.

If at First You Don't Succeed . . .

At antiques shows, consider rearranging some of your merchandise at least every day. Making changes periodically throughout the day would be even better. This is particularly important for merchandise at the front of your booth.

Although different shoppers will be attending the show each day, your fellow show dealers will be there for the duration. During the course of the show, they may walk past your booth numerous times. Rearranging your merchandise gives them a new reason to stop and look.

A dealer who specializes in pattern glass might have missed your miniature Westward Ho mug earlier. However, he might see it the second time through when it's in a new spot. A few cosmetic changes to the overall appearance of your display might be all it takes to get him into your booth that second time.

fall in love with the same piece he passed by only a week ago. Last week it was in a different place and either unseen or unappreciated in that context.

Ask the dealer whose Noritake berry bowl and matching dishes sat unnoticed on a cupboard shelf for months. The day after he moved the set onto a tabletop at the front of his booth, it sold. All it took was a more visible location.

24 Use Effective Lighting

WHEN IT'S BARELY SEEN, IT'S RARELY SOLD.

Once upon a time, Goldilocks went antiquing. She walked into the first booth and tried to look around, but it was *to-o-o-o* dark. She walked into the second booth and started to look around, but it was *to-o-o-o* bright. She walked into the third booth and began to look around, and it was *just* right. Goldi felt comfortable shopping in the booth and even found a chair to replace one she'd broken the previous week.

The lighting in your booth isn't a make-believe concern. It's a key factor in any effective display. A well-lit booth invites the customer in and makes his shopping experience enjoyable. A booth that is either too dark or too bright can make him uncomfortable. Antsy shoppers won't be thinking about your merchandise. Instead, they'll focus on getting in and out as quickly as possible.

Proper lighting can also set the mood for a sale. More importantly, it enables your customers to see your merchandise. That sounds pretty basic, but everything else depends on it. If your string of sleigh bells is hidden in shadows, it's not likely to sell.

Some antique shops are notorious for being as dark as the inside of a whale's belly. At one mall, a woman literally shopped by flashlight. She deftly shone the beam into the dark recesses of shelves and the murky areas under tables. She solved the problem; it's just unfortunate she had to do so.

Finding the merchandise is only the first step. The customer still needs adequate lighting if he wants to examine an item. If he has to squint to check for hairline cracks on a majolica asparagus server, he may think twice about purchasing the piece.

Adequate lighting is also needed for merchandise in your showcases. If you use unlit cases, take full advantage of ambient lighting. Sheet music

▶ FYI

Lighting options:

1. Place items in windows to take advantage of sunlight
2. Use mirrors to reflect available light
3. Turn on lamps that are for sale
4. Add lights under tables to highlight merchandise there
5. Add free-standing floodlights
6. Install track lighting

Additional lighting greatly improved this display of sewer tile. Lights on both sides accented the detailed pattern of the carved bookcase, while overhead track lights illuminated the merchandise on the shelves.

and doilies placed on top of a showcase can block the light and obstruct the customer's view.

Harsh or excessive lighting can be as detrimental as too little lighting. Customers may feel like suspects in an interrogation room. "So, Mr. Smith, you want to buy the vase. That's fine. But first, why don't you answer a few questions. Where were you on the night of the fifth? . . ." Again, uneasy customers make reluctant buyers.

When installing lights, keep them out of the line of sight. Your customers will not appreciate being blinded by bare bulbs. Additionally, bright lights create glare. It will be difficult to sell your Deer & Pine Tree finger bowl if the glare makes it impossible for your customers to distinguish the pattern.

Where there is smoke, there is fire; and, where there is light, there is heat. Heat can wreak havoc on plastics and other materials. Metal objects may become too hot to handle if placed close to a light source. You don't want your customers playing hot potato with your chrome-plated Art Deco ashtray. Keep it a safe distance from heat-producing lamps.

Give Me a Light!

Pay particular attention to lighting conditions at antique shows.

Indoor shows require artificial lighting, which may not create optimal viewing conditions. Halogen lights, fluorescent lights, and incandescent lights will change the apparent color of your merchandise. Artificial lighting may also cause headaches, blurred vision, and fatigue.

If you use tripods, they should be sturdy enough to hold the light and stable enough that they don't tip over. Put the stands where customers won't bump into them. Be sure to secure the cords to prevent accidents.

Whenever possible, let your customer examine merchandise in natural lighting. Sunlight shows an item's true colors. It also helps the buyer detect damage. Hairline cracks that are hardly noticeable in moderate lighting can be seen clearly in bright sunlight.

During outdoor shows, consider the movement of the sun. Your paint-decorated balloon-back chair and your walnut jelly cupboard might be in the sunshine in the morning. But, as the sun crosses the sky, the shadow from your cupboard might envelop the chair, obscuring its detailed design.

Take an objective look at your booth. Critically examine the lighting in every section, checking for shadows and dark recesses. Then study your merchandise. Would your Heywood-Wakefield wicker rocker have a better chance of selling if the lighting was improved? Pair it with your floor lamp. A lit lamp creates an inviting, warm glow that says, "I'd look cozy in your living room." At the same time, it's highlighting the craftsmanship of your rocking chair.

Remember that the amount of light outside affects the lighting inside your shop or mall. Ask the mall manager to turn on your lamps during

Color, shape, and design will be accentuated when your glassware is placed in front of a window or backlit by artificial lights.

Position your merchandise to take advantage of the light available to you. When this George Husher storage jar is displayed so light from a window rakes across the surface, the impressed name is more visible.

dismal, rainy days. You may also need additional lighting during the morning or evening hours. If possible, put some of your "for sale" lamps on timers.

Take full advantage of any natural lighting you have. An open shelving unit in front of a window is a perfect display piece for colored glassware. Your cobalt Moderntone Sailboat dishes will look unimpressive sitting in a cupboard along a dark wall. However, that dinnerware will stand out when placed on a windowsill and backlit by the sun.

Sunlight can also emphasize certain features of items other than glassware. It can accent the graining in a piece of furniture or highlight an impressed mark on a piece of stoneware. Highlight unique characteristics of merchandise with natural lighting whenever possible.

Lights Out

You've heard the old joke—Where was the cat when the lights went out? In the dark.

You don't want to leave your customers in the dark either. You've worked hard to provide lighting that allows them to see and examine your merchandise. Don't ruin the effect by turning off your lights fifteen minutes before closing. Leave overhead lights and smaller lamps on until the last customer has finished shopping.

Be courteous. A customer browsing late in the day deserves the same consideration as someone shopping over his lunch hour. Turning off the lights tells your shopper you're in a hurry and have better things to do than wait on him. Tattooing the words *GET OUT!* on your forehead or announcing that the attack dogs have been let loose will achieve the same result—the customer will run for the door.

25 Accent Clear Glassware

BUCK NAKED AND NO ONE NOTICED.

Clear glassware is a victim of the Invisible Man syndrome. People look right past it and right through it, not even realizing it's there. Take a lesson from the Invisible Man—dress it up. You can't sell what isn't noticed.

Clear glassware is often overlooked because it doesn't stand out against the background. Make it noticeable. Colors attract the eye. You'll quickly spot a bright-red beach ball on a shoreline or a neon sign beside a dark highway. Likewise, shoppers will notice your clear glassware when you incorporate colors into the display. Put pink confetti in a wine glass or multi-colored jelly beans in a crystal candy container.

Colored props can also be used to highlight the decorative elements of clear glassware. The intricate pattern of your Cameo cocktail shaker will really stand out when the piece is filled with green confetti. Displaying your Fostoria Meadow Rose torte plate on a piece of purple velvet will emphasize its delicate etching.

Using colored props is not the only way to highlight clear glass. Even something as simple as displaying glassware in a prominent location can attract attention. Few shoppers will notice your Orchid nut bowls if they're displayed at the bottom of a dark shelving unit. Put them on your cherry serving cart and they will be snapped up before you can say, "Take me out to the ball game."

Special lighting can also be used to accent glassware. A spotlight aimed at your Hawkes cut glass pitcher highlights the facets. Add a mirror and the effect is dazzling.

Accenting clear glassware is a relatively simple idea. But, choosing which technique to use does require some forethought. Select props that are least likely to damage your merchandise. Colored rocks might be appropriate in your glass minnow trap, but they can chip, crack, or scratch your Borden's malt jar.

Consider your customer. If your Twisted Optic preserve dish is full of packing peanuts, he'll be performing all manner of wild contortions trying to check the bottom of the piece for damage.

Customers do the craziest things, and you should expect the unexpected. An absentminded professor might scatter marbles across the floor if he turns your Paneled Forget-Me-Not spooner upside-down looking for a mark. Use common sense when determining how to accent a particular piece: it might be appropriate to simply spotlight the spooner in this instance.

▶ FYI

Props that accent clear glassware:

1. Colored tissue
2. Packing peanuts
3. Excelsior
4. Confetti
5. Marbles
6. Food (peanuts in a peanut jar)
7. Special backdrops
8. Spotlights
9. Mirrors

Use a variety of props to draw attention to your otherwise unremarkable clear glassware. Tissue paper emphasizes the frosted design on a juice glass, while colored paper and excelsior make the wine glass and creamer stand out on a shelf.

26 Display Art as Art

EVERY GENUINE WORK OF ART HAS AS MUCH REASON FOR BEING AS THE EARTH AND SUN.

—*Ralph Waldo Emerson*

Emerson was on to something. Any true piece of art deserves admiration and respect. Simple enough. Visit The Metropolitan Museum of Art in New York, and you'll find art displayed in glorious fashion. The same atmosphere exists at most art galleries. Gallery owners are experts at creating aesthetic displays that appeal to potential buyers.

Art isn't just for the snooty tea-party types who glide through galleries with their noses in the air and their French poodles in their arms. ("I'll take the Peale.") It's also enjoyed by the beer-swilling construction worker who's more at home in a wholesale club than a country club. ("Hey, Bud! You got any Elvis on black velvet?")

Stereotypes maybe, but the point is clear. Art transcends definition. One man's trash is another man's art, and all pieces deserve to be treated like masterpieces. Unfortunately, that's not the way it works in the antiques industry. Haphazard placement is the rule rather than the exception.

You're familiar with the scene—paintings stacked against the wall and framed prints crammed in cardboard boxes. These display techniques do little to impress a potential buyer. Actually, how can the merchandise even begin to interest him? He can't *see* it.

If it doesn't deserve to be properly displayed, it probably shouldn't be in your booth. Make the artist proud. Take time to create a display that will showcase the work. Your customer isn't going to take home your Currier and Ives print and toss it behind the sofa. He's going to proudly display it

▶ FYI

Types of artwork:

1. Original paintings and drawings
2. Prints and etchings
3. Posters
4. Photographs
5. Animated cels
6. Sculptures
7. Bronzes
8. Wood carvings
9. Pottery
10. Art glass
11. Tapestries
12. Needlework

An Apple a Day . . .

Teach your customers, and teach them well. Take advantage of every opportunity to educate your clientele. Provide detailed information about the artwork in your displays. Note the artist's name, nationality, and birth and death dates. You might list other pertinent information, such as where he received his training, where he exhibited his works, and what awards he won. Check your library's reference section for books profiling recognized artists. *Who's Who in American Art* and Mantle Fielding's *Dictionary of American Painters, Sculptors & Engravers* are particularly helpful. Local art guilds and state museums can provide information on lesser-known local artists.

above the mantel. When you hang the print as part of a room setting, you're helping him to visualize the piece in his own home.

Artwork will sell more quickly when it's appropriately displayed. A Boehm capped chickadee sculpture that's been gathering dust in an old fruit crate for months might sell in just a few days once it's highlighted in your booth. For the most part, your customer will assume that items prominently displayed are worth more than the pieces stacked beside your cannonball rope bed or piled on the floor. He might unroll the "East of Eden" movie poster he found in a nail keg in your booth and think it's only worth $50. Frame it and hang it on the wall, and he'll agree it's a $150 piece.

Valuable and important pieces of art deserve special attention. It doesn't make sense to carelessly hang a $1,200 painting on a rusty wrought-iron gate. But, that's just what one dealer did. His lack of concern suggested the painting was not valuable. Why should his customers think otherwise?

A stack of artwork in a box doesn't entice the customer. Presenting art in an attractive manner allows shoppers to appreciate its artistic merit.

27 Check the Overall Appearance

SCORE BIG WITH A LITTLE RAZZLE-DAZZLE.

You're familiar with the scene—booths that look like they were arranged by someone with a scoop shovel. Merchandise is everywhere, mostly in piles on the floor. Furniture has items stacked on and around it. Nothing seems to be in any specific spot for any particular reason.

Customers who are compulsively neat can only avert their eyes and walk away. Those brave enough to venture into the booth may feel overwhelmed or claustrophobic. Haphazard, unorderly placement does little to encourage sales, particularly if smaller items are buried or unnoticed because they are lost in the clutter.

Ask any marching band member. If you play exceptionally well but your ranks aren't straight, you won't win the contest. If your alignment is precision-perfect but your music is off-tempo and out of tune, you won't win the contest. Judges don't just look at the marching or only listen to the music. They evaluate the entire performance—the overall effect.

So do your customers. Even if your art glass display is spectacular, customers will give you low scores if your board games are merely tossed in a pile on the floor. Look at the big picture. Present all of your merchandise in a pleasing, unified manner. Everything should work together to create an atmosphere conducive to shopping.

One interesting display may attract a customer to your booth. But, it's the overall appearance that will have the greatest impact on whether he spends time looking at anything else. Messiness can lose a sale because your

FYI

Ways to improve overall appearance:

1 If you use carpeting, rugs, or mats, make sure the edges are securely anchored. In addition to being a hazard, untidy rugs make the display area look second-rate.

2 If you use mirrors as props in your displays, don't overdo it. Too many mirrors focus attention on reflections rather than merchandise.

3 Avoid using mirrored props that are cracked or chipped. If you must, then arrange them where the damage is least likely to be noticed.

4 Take advantage of what you do have. Put colored glass in a window where it can catch the sun.

5 Attract attention with non-antique items. One shop owner used blooming amaryllis to accent primitive furniture in his front window.

customer believes that sloppiness carries over into other parts of your business. A CEO for a major airline summed it up in this fashion: "If we have coffee stains on our fold-down lap trays, the passenger assumes we don't know how to do our engine maintenance." The same holds true for your business. If your displays are unorganized, why should the customer assume your bookwork is any different? Did you charge the right price? Did you write the ticket correctly?

Avoid a cluttered, disorganized appearance. Make the customer's job as easy as possible. He doesn't want to paw through a bushel basket of stuffed animals on the off chance that a Snoopy Astronaut doll landed there. Display Snoopy where he can readily be seen, and you'll send a rabid Peanuts collector into orbit.

Your booth is not a dumping ground for merchandise. That's what landfills are for. You aren't selling garbage; you're selling quality antiques and collectibles. And you're proud to be doing so. Your displays should reflect that sense of pride. Space may be at a premium, but there's no reason your displays have to announce the fact. If you've got a hole in your display of Warwick china, rework the display. Don't put your Ballerina Barbie and Gene Autry cast-iron cap pistol there just so the spot will be filled.

Develop a game plan for creating effective displays. That plan should include some idea of how to arrange large and small items in relation to each other. Do you really want your 1950s Tonka towtruck in your cherry corner cupboard, or would your set of Carnival glass berry bowls make more sense there?

Place items in their natural settings, using smalls to accentuate larger

The Gotta-Get-Their-Attention Blues

Color, like a magnet, can either attract or repel. Yellow is seen from a greater distance than any other color and is also remembered longer than any other. Conversely, most blues are not seen at a distance and do not attract attention.

Some colors are associated with quality, others are not; some enhance the merchandise, others detract from its appeal. Purple is a color traditionally associated with royalty. Use it to emphasize your more elegant items. On the other hand, brown table covers will do little to emphasize red glassware. Understand, a color that works well with one type of merchandise may not be appropriate for another. Experiment to see what works.

Use the right colors, and you can encourage shoppers to spend more time in your booth. Red produces feelings of warmth and nearness; blue creates feelings of coolness and airiness. Both can be used to create a comfortable environment for your customer.

▶ FYI

Items to consider when using tablecovers:

1 Avoid wild patterns. Merchandise will be lost in the visual confusion.

2 Avoid white and pale colors. They show wear more quickly and will soon look grubby.

3 Use colors that coordinate with your merchandise. Rose and teal are Victorian colors; orange is not.

4 Use tablecovers that are long enough to reach the floor. Customers should be looking at the merchandise *on* the table, not the cartons, bags, and extra stock stored under it.

5 If your tablecovers have unfinished borders, roll them under. Loose threads, raveling edges, and messages on the selvage are distracting and unprofessional.

6 Consider the wind when setting up outdoors. Be sure your covers are weighted or attached to the table in some way.

pieces. Arrange your Meakin dishes on a table and use a vase, complete with flowers, as a centerpiece. Display advertising tins in a cupboard. Put a candlestick and book on a nightstand. Place gloves in a glovebox and display the glovebox on a dresser.

Make sure small items aren't lost in the display. Few customers will notice your Cracker Jack pencil clip if there's a Mickey Mouse pop-up book on one side of it and a Blondie Goes to Leisureland game on the other. Instead, group a number of small items together so they are not over-

Looks Can Kill

Your merchandise is judged by the company it keeps. That means you. Right or wrong, customers develop attitudes about your business based on what you wear and how you look. A Harley T-shirt and faded blue jeans might be appropriate for attending a farm auction, but it's not the attire most customers want to see when you're dusting your merchandise. Moreover, if you haven't shaved in two days and spaghetti sauce from lunch is still on your chin, your customer might be reluctant to conduct business with you.

Customers also form opinions about your merchandise based on the decor of the establishment and the condition the building is in. Use Purple Passion paint on the walls, and your customers will spend more time marveling at your color choice than studying your merchandise. If your customer sees a water-marked ceiling, rickety staircases, and exposed electrical wires, he's only going to be concerned with getting out before the wrecking ball arrives. If your facility is attractive and well cared for, customers will focus on your merchandise rather than the surroundings.

whelmed by the larger pieces. Put your pencil clip on a pencil and place it with your Mickey Mouse fountain pen and Blondie stationery. In the right display, these pieces will really draw attention.

Placement of children's furniture also requires special consideration. A child's rocker will look out of place when displayed next to a step-back cupboard because both pieces are not the same scale. Putting the rocker with your bentwood cradle and placing your maple butcher's block beside the cupboard creates a more sensible display.

Creating attractive displays takes time and effort. Don't ruin the effect. Paraphernalia casually added—decorations, signs, baskets of flowers, etc.—can effectively camouflage the merchandise. You're not trying to sell your "20% Off" signs. Don't place them where they detract from the items on display.

It is possible to have too much of a good thing. Excessive cleverness is the enemy of effective merchandising. It makes the vehicle memorable and the ride memorable, but the product is left sputtering in the dust. Remember, you're not trying to make your customer laugh or applaud. You're trying to influence him to buy your product. Use signs and decorative material in moderation.

IV The Enhanced Display

Creating a display involves more than just grouping items together. To be effective, displays must combine merchandise, props, and information in an appealing manner. They must attract attention, but not detract from the merchandise.

A few packages and bows or a small decorated tree will put your customers in a festive mood at Christmas. But if the tree is so large it blocks their view of your booth, if your electronic chimes blare the same carols over and over, and if multicolored lights are flashing in every display, dumbfounded customers will notice only your props.

Merchandise itself can be overwhelming if it's displayed poorly. How many times have you seen a mountain of glassware just shoved on a table? Nothing is sorted by color or pattern. Tea cups are on one end of the table; the matching saucers are on the other. An ocean of unmatched plates, bowls, and serving pieces is in between. Depending on your mood and how much energy you have, you might take the time to search through everything. Then again, you might not. The same is true of your customer.

Unfortunately, dealers who use this pile-it-on technique are overlooking a variety of ways to promote their merchandise. Arranging glassware by color is visually attractive and captures the customer's attention. Grouping like items together makes it easier to locate a specific pattern. Including a shelf-talker with a selection of Heisey provides the customer with some historical information about the company. Adding a Depression glass reference book allows novice collectors to learn more about your merchandise. And, promoting candlesticks and wine glasses as wedding presents provides the customer with an alternative to traditional retail stores.

28 Create Shelf-Talkers

GIVE YOUR MERCHANDISE A VOICE OF ITS OWN.

Imagine walking into a grocery store and discovering someone had removed the labels from all the cans. The sign above your head reads "Soup," but you don't know if the cans in front of you contain split pea, tomato, or chunky chicken. To further complicate matters, you don't know if you're looking at a generic product or one made by Campbell's.

Labels are wonderful things. They tell what type of soup is in a can, the estimated gas mileage of a new Saturn coupe, and the care instructions for a cashmere sweater. They make shopping easier by helping the consumer to make informed decisions.

As a dealer, you can assist your shoppers by enhancing your displays with shelf-talkers—informational cards that are placed with the merchandise. Shelf-talkers enable the display itself to answer certain anticipated questions, such as "Does this player piano work?" and "Is Van Briggle pottery still being made?"

Shelf-talkers can provide information about a specific item or an entire display. A card with your Adlake switch lock might explain that it's marked NYC, which stands for New York Central Railroad. A shelf-talker with your Occupied Japan display might mention those items were produced from the end of World War II until April 1952.

Emphasize a special item by placing it with a shelf-talker. This Overbeck squirrel is accompanied by a shelf-talker providing historical information on the pottery.

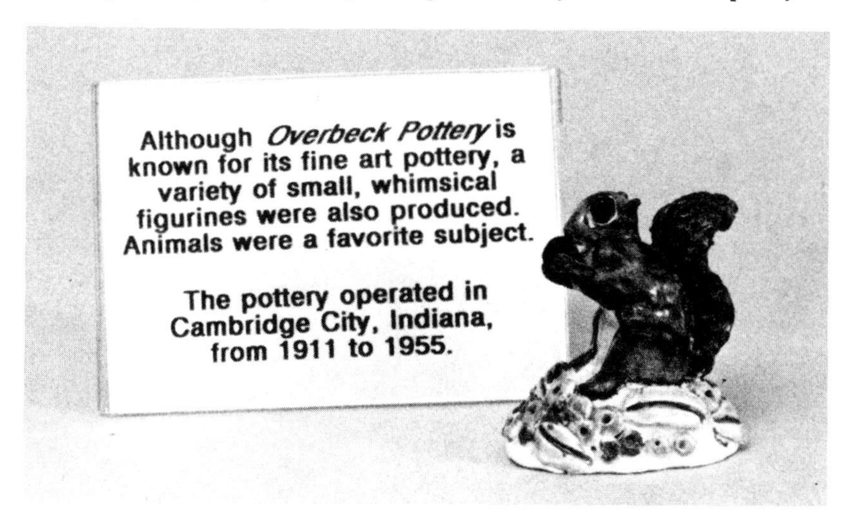

Few and Far Between

Use shelf-talkers sparingly—to highlight unusual or obscure merchandise or to draw attention to a specific display. If you add too many shelf-talkers, your customer will be overwhelmed and will read just a few, if any.

Make sure the information you provide is both relevant and important. Don't waste time with trivialities. A shelf-talker can note that your eagle woodcarving was made by a runaway slave, but there's no need to mention that his wife died of consumption.

Shelf-talkers are excellent promotional tools because they supply product information. A customer who knows relatively little about your merchandise might be reluctant to ask questions. Someone intrigued by your stereo viewer might not know how it is used or when it was popular. A shelf-talker could answer both questions.

Consumers like to feel they know something about their purchases, and many will be impressed by your knowledge. Providing detailed information about a particular item demonstrates you are not only knowledgeable but also reputable. A shopper may be more inclined to buy your copy of John Steinbeck's *The Red Pony* when he knows it's a limited-edition signed by the author.

You can use shelf-talkers to explain how an item works and what it was used for, tell when it was made, and give its history. One dealer used shelf-talkers with his display of pottery to give a brief overview of each company represented. Another dealer used shelf-talkers to list the authors and illustrators of his children's books.

Although shelf-talkers can enhance your credibility with a customer, an incorrect shelf-talker can be detrimental. Always verify your information. Your shelf-talker might state that Rookwood Pottery is no longer produced; a knowledgeable pottery collector will know better. Should he believe the rest of your shelf-talkers? Once you've lost his trust, you're likely to lose his business.

Creative shelf-talkers encourage your customer to spend more time in your booth. The longer you hold his attention, the more likely you are to make a sale. Use an interesting shelf-talker to explain the different types of snowdomes you have on display. Even if he doesn't buy anything this time around, he'll at least remember your booth.

Of course, shelf-talkers must be legible to be effective. If you make them by hand, print clearly. Your customer will ignore them if he can't read the

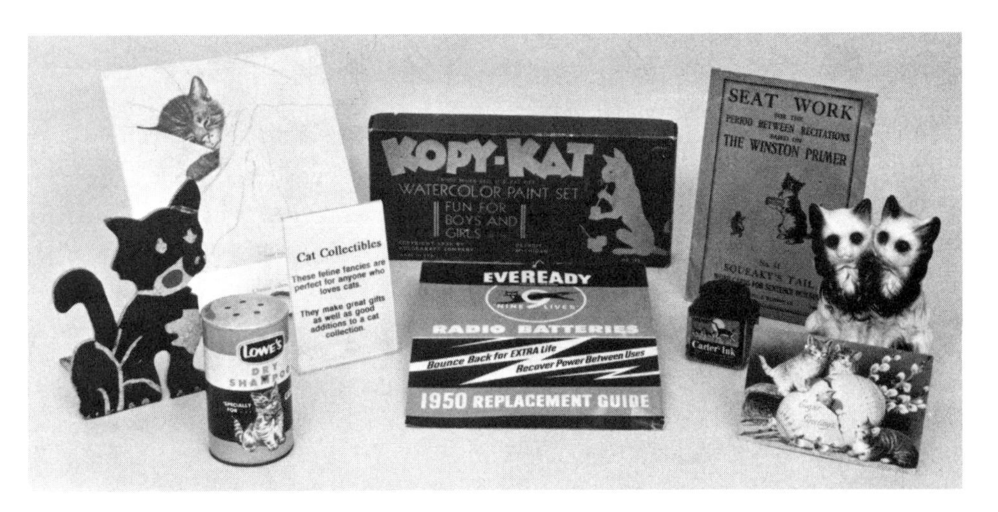

A shelf-talker ties together the diversified items in this display of cat collectibles. The shelf-talker reads, "Cat Collectibles—These feline fancies are perfect for anyone who loves cats. They make great gifts as well as good additions to a cat collection."

▶ FYI

Tips for creating shelf-talkers:

1 There's no standard format for making or using a shelf-talker. Adjust the type and style to best fit your needs.

2 Shelf-talkers can be printed by hand, typed, or created with a desktop publishing system.

3 Self-standing acrylic frames make excellent holders for shelf-talkers. Write the information on a piece of paper large enough to fit the frame.

4 Creating a shelf-talker can be as easy as folding a stiff piece of paper in half. Set the paper on the table, creased edge up, to form a tent. Write the information on one side.

5 Use an eye-catching color that doesn't overpower the merchandise. A medium yellow works well in most cases. White doesn't attract attention, and dark colors make the text difficult to read.

6 Shelf-talkers should be large enough to be noticed, but small enough that they don't overwhelm. $3\frac{1}{2}$ inches by 5 inches works well in most cases.

7 Keep your shelf-talkers simple. If they are too elaborate, they will draw attention away from the items they accompany.

8 A shelf-talker doesn't have to sit on a shelf. It can be placed on top of your partner's desk or hung beside your John J. Audubon print.

handwriting. Consider typing your shelf-talkers. Or, if you have a computer, you might want to buy a desktop publishing program. Some relatively inexpensive software packages can help you create professional, attractive shelf-talkers.

Keep in mind that shelf-talkers are only one component of the overall display. They should enhance the merchandise, not detract from it. To be effective, they must be visible. One thoughtful mall dealer placed shelf-talkers with his display of pocket watches. Each card provided information about the watch: who made it, when it was made, the quality of gold in the case, the type of movement, and the price. Each card was typed and legible. Up to that point, he'd done everything right. But, instead of putting the cards beside the watches, he placed them *underneath* the watches, covering much of the information he so diligently prepared.

29 Design Professional Signs

ENLIST THE AID OF A SILENT PARTNER.

You're whizzing down the highway at 65 miles per hour. Your wife is badgering you to attend the Peterson's masquerade ball on Friday. Your kids are bickering in the back seat and beating the heck out of each other. Your dog is barking at every blonde you pass. Everyone is competing for your attention.

What's a billboard to do? To be effective, it must catch your eye, make you want to read the message, and, most difficult of all, present information in a clear and concise manner. Time is of the essence. In only a few seconds, you, the wife, the kids, and the dog will be long gone—answering the call of the next beckoning billboard.

At times it will be necessary to place signs in your shop or booth. Take a lesson from a billboard. Use signs that grab the customer's attention, make him want to read the message, and present information in a simple manner.

The appearance of your sign and the way in which its message is presented will determine whether your customer reads and understands it. If the lettering is too small, he won't be able to read it. If there is too much text, he won't take the time to read it. And, if the sign is poorly located, he won't even be able to see it.

A form of overgrown shelf-talker, signs can be used to provide information about your large pieces of merchandise. A small shelf-talker might be lost next to your mahogany backbar, but a bright, informative sign could really stand out.

Likewise, the size of the display itself might necessitate the use of a sign

A Place of Their Own

Give special consideration to where you place your signs. Put them in highly visible locations where they attract the customer's attention without detracting from the merchandise. In one mall, a sign for a holiday sale was taped to the front of a showcase, unintentionally blocking the customer's view of the Easter postcards, blown-glass eggs, and papier mâché candy container.

Place each sign so it is apparent which merchandise it is paired with. If your sign says "50% off all items this shelf," make sure the customer knows which shelf is referred to. When the sign is taped to the front of a shelf, it's particularly confusing. What's on sale? The matchholders above the sign or the milk bottles below it?

rather than a shelf-talker. A large sign would be a more effective way of highlighting the seven gasoline pumps you have for sale. A simple shelf-talker would be dwarfed by the giants.

Like most household cleaners, signs are multipurpose. They can do more than just provide information about your merchandise. Use attractive signs to outline specific shop or mall policies. Tell your customer which charge cards are accepted, remind him of the layaway plan, outline the discount policy, or advertise a sale. Anticipate your customer's questions. Use a sign to direct them to another room of antiques or to lead the way to the restroom.

Signs are an extension of both your shop and your individual displays. Make them presentable. Many a signmaker's greatest error comes in being too fanciful. Simplicity is best. Your calligraphy "Sale" sign definitely stands out, but if your customer can't tell your 2s from your 5s, he'll wonder if your merchandise is 20 percent off or 50 percent off. He'll wish he had a

Your signs create a lasting impression. These examples present the same information, but one sign is definitely more professional than the other. Which would you rather place in your shop?

Calligraphy/English dictionary. Plain, bold lettering prevents confusion. Use a thick, black marker or a desktop publishing program to create signs that are legible.

Remember, everything your customer sees influences his impression of you and your merchandise. If your signs are sloppy, he may think you

Common Courtesy Counts

Good business etiquette says you wouldn't dream of being rude to your customer. Neither should your signs. Make them brief and courteous. Follow the example of one thoughtful dealer who displayed a group of light-up advertising clocks and provided a surge protector so they could be tested. The accompanying sign read: "Test clocks here. Unplug when done. Thanks." It was neatly lettered, to-the-point, and located where it didn't block the customer's view of the clocks. Most importantly, it thanked the customer for returning the display to its original condition.

The sign with this small basket of linens is insulting. It suggests the dealer doesn't care about his customer. He's only concerned with minimizing the amount of work he has to do in his booth.

aren't a competent antiques dealer, you don't know much about your merchandise, and your prices are too high. (No one said his thought processes are rational.)

One dealer used a sign to promote a line of paste wax he'd used on the furniture in his booth. The thought was commendable; the implementation was abominable. Using a fine-point pen, he'd scrawled his advertising pitch on a piece of corrugated cardboard and laid it on a tabletop. He'd created a monster. His sign, like Bigfoot, was rarely seen and never understood. A neatly lettered, professional-looking sign would have done the job.

30 Demand Accuracy

BE RIGHT WHEN YOU WRITE.

No doubt, the laughter coming from the next room was another customer who had noticed the tag on a piece of treenware. It read, "Large wooden bowel."

Of course, that's not what the dealer meant. After all, there's a bit of a difference between a bowl and a bowel. Call it a simple printing error or call it a spelling mistake. It doesn't matter. Someone messed up. Though the dealer might have caused a few chuckles, he probably lost some credibility as well.

Customers form opinions about you and your merchandise based on the accuracy of the information you provide. Accurate information can strengthen trust and foster a continued business relationship. Incorrect information can breed distrust and foul future sales. Boopie may look a lot like Candlewick, but it's not. When a glass buyer finds a Boopie goblet labeled Candlewick, he'll question the dealer's knowledge or integrity. Since the glassware is incorrectly tagged, he'll wonder if it's mispriced as well.

Class Is in Session

Pay particular attention to spelling, grammar, and punctuation when making tags and signs. If you are trying to sell a "pear of bowls," will the customer have much faith in the correctness of anything else in your booth?

Spelling errors are probably the most common mistakes. They are also the easiest to correct. Use a dictionary if you are unsure of a word. The proper spelling of company names and product lines can be checked in a general price guide. It only takes a few seconds to verify that Wedgwood is spelled with one "e" or that the name of the pottery line is "Fiesta," not "Festia." Your merchandise can even provide some of the answers. The dealer who offered a "potatoe chips tin" should have checked the label.

Grammar and punctuation are especially important. If your sign says "No layaways excepted, in this booth," you've given your customer a double dose of poor English. A perceptive shopper will know your sign doesn't make the grade. The comma is unnecessary, and "excepted" should have been "accepted."

Additionally, the sign on your row of showcases should read "Don't open cases," not "Don't open case's." Actually, both sound bossy; try "Please ask for assistance." If grammar isn't your strong suit, buy an English handbook. *The Elements of Style* by William Strunk, Jr. and E.B. White is one particularly good example.

The ABCs of Curious Customers

Quiz time—again. A customer just asked you a question, but you don't know the answer. You should:

- **a** Just say anything. He won't know the difference.
- **b** Say, "Listen, Slick, I just sell the stuff."
- **c** Politely admit you don't know the answer.

The correct answer is "c." Making up a story (answer "a") will hurt you in the long run once the customer learns the truth. Being rude (answer "b") will hurt you immediately because the customer might just leave.

Honesty is still the best policy. Be polite. Tell your customer he asked a good question, but admit you don't know the answer. If you have reference material available, try to find the answer for him. Show him you are willing to do a little research. You will have taken a big step toward winning his loyalty.

If you can't provide the answer, refer your customer to a someone who might know. You can also suggest an appropriate reference book. Making the extra effort to assist him allows you to demonstrate your customer service.

If you're unsure about an item, don't guess. Your shot in the dark may misfire, emphasizing your ignorance. Take the extra time to find the right answer, whether it's determining the type of fabric used in a vintage wedding gown or the kind of wood in a chest of drawers.

Your third-grade teacher was right: spelling *is* important. Misspellings and poor grammar can stereotype you as ignorant and unreliable. Most customers won't pass up your Fulper bean pot simply because the tag says "Fulpher." However, they may feel more comfortable buying from a straight-A speller.

Their logic goes something like this: If you don't know the difference between "metal" and "medal"—or aren't concerned enough to be sure you're accurate—you probably don't know the difference between cut glass and pressed glass, between oak and tiger maple, and between an antique and a reproduction.

Keep in mind: the bigger they are, the harder they fall. The more expensive your merchandise, the more noticeable your mistakes become. If a customer sees a "Clearnce Sale" sign at a flea market, he might laugh it off, mumbling "Buy a vowel!" But a mistake at a major show leaves a lasting impression. If a $36,000 circa-1800 secretary is tagged "New Hamshire," the customer might think the dealer is careless or geographically illiterate.

31 Identify Solds, Holds, and Layaways

WHEN IT'S GOING . . . GOING . . . BUT NOT QUITE GONE.

You're in trouble. The man in your booth has lust in his eyes. He's stroking your pie safe. Running his hands along the tiger maple. Caressing the unique dog-motif punched tins. Tracing his fingers up and down the turned legs. Gazing longingly at the dovetailed construction. Sighing contentedly. A man in love.

Now he's headed your way. Walking briskly. Smiling. He glances over his shoulder at the object of his affection, then turns back to you and breathlessly says, "Your pie safe is *wonderful!* But I didn't see a price. How much is it?"

You'd rather be anywhere else right now. You're about to shred his heart. If only you'd remembered to tag the piece "Sold" this morning. You think to yourself, "I'm such an idiot!"

Let your customer know when an item is sold. Individual "Sold" tags are used on each piece in this special holding area. Extra emphasis is provided by a shelf-talker stating, "Sorry! Someone beat you to it. Items in this area are already sold."

"Uh, well . . ." you stumble for the right words. How do you break it to him gently? You grit your teeth and say, "It's kinda sold." It doesn't matter what else you say; he's not listening. His eyes glaze over. He stares blankly at his feet. He mumbles something, you're not sure what, and shuffles back to the booth. A man in mourning.

Don't taunt your customers. When an item is sold, simply removing the price tag does more harm than good. Once you've frustrated or angered an interested customer, nothing else matters. He won't look at the rest of your merchandise if he's got a bad attitude. Don't hold your breath. He won't be buying anything.

That's unfortunate, because items that are already sold can actually encourage sales. When an item is sold but not immediately removed from your shop or booth, place a "Sold" tag on it. This tag lets your customer know the item is no longer for sale. It also tells him your merchandise is worth buying. A little voice in his head says, "This cupboard was a good buy. Now it's sold. Don't hesitate if you see something you like."

Merchandise that is no longer for sale requires special attention. Don't leave sold/hold/layaway items on your display floor for an extended period of time. These pieces, especially furniture, take up room that can best be devoted to other inventory. Remove the item and bring in new merchandise or rearrange the display to create a new look.

When you relocate sold/hold/layaway items, don't just put them anywhere. Keep your customer in mind. One mall put "hold" merchandise in a front window by the cash register, teasing passers-by with goods they couldn't purchase. Because there were no special "hold" tags or signs,

Nightmare on Mall Street

At one mall, not-for-sale merchandise was moved to a special room. The customer who purchased a Duncan Phyfe-style table and chairs slept easily that night, secure in the belief that his $250 investment would be safe until he could return that weekend to pick it up.

Not even in his wildest dreams could he have imagined the sight that greeted him. One table. Four chairs. Just what he'd paid for. But wait! There's more. Miscellaneous scratches. Deep gouges. A battered and abused piece of furniture.

Lacking a degree in nuclear physics, the dealer had stood the chairs on the table. He was, however, able to add two and two and deduce that he was on the losing end of the equation. Not only did he have an angry customer, he also had to pay to have the tabletop professionally refinished.

▶ FYI

What to do with items that are not for sale:

1 Small props: If you want to keep your plate stand for future use, tag it "for display only." If not, the shopper who buys your Knowles "Over the Rainbow" plate will assume it goes with the piece.

2 Large props: Display pieces, such as your curved-glass china cabinet, should be clearly tagged "not for sale." Otherwise, confused customers will want to know the price.

3 Exhibits: Even though it isn't for sale, your collection of political memorabilia may make an interesting display at election time. Separate it from the rest of your merchandise and clearly label it "Special Display—Items courtesy of . . ."

shoppers who asked about the items were frustrated when they learned the pieces weren't for sale.

If possible, designate one spot as a holding area for merchandise that has already been sold. Clearly identify both the area and the merchandise. Customers will know the items aren't for sale, and you will know where the merchandise is located when the buyer returns to pick it up.

Placing items in a holding area prevents customers from handling them. The person who put your $800 Cherry Smash dispenser on layaway won't be pleased if some idly curious customer chips it. When the buyer makes his last payment, he expects the dispenser to be in the same condition as when he first saw it. Until the merchandise leaves your shop, you are responsible for it. Do what you can to keep it from being damaged or stolen.

32 Provide Reference Material

BOOK 'EM, DANNO!

The man holding your creamware baby's plate is frowning. The longer he looks at that piece of pottery, the deeper the frown becomes. He's hearing voices in his head.

One voice is calling him unflattering names. "You idiot!" it screams. "How could you have left the Roseville book at home? How are you going to decide if this unmarked piece is really Roseville or just some well-made imitation?"

The other is a kinder, gentler voice. "Sure, the piece is Roseville," it reassures him. "It looks like Roseville. It feels like Roseville. If it walks like a duck and talks like a duck . . ."

The voices only confuse him. He'll buy the plate if he's sure it's Roseville. But he has no way of determining whether it is. If only you had a Roseville book he could borrow. But you don't. The piece of creamware goes back into your display. The sale goes down the drain.

Providing reference material with your displays is an excellent way to boost confidence and promote goodwill. More than that, it can create sales. Your unmarked creamware might have been part of a Roseville juvenile set. That pottery-buying customer would have bought it if he had been able to

A price guide for cameras is an excellent addition to this display. It provides instant reference material for shoppers. A shelf-talker notes, "For your convenience, a copy of* McKeown's Price Guide to Cameras *is provided for you to browse through. Thank you for returning it to the display so others may use it."

Use Only as Directed

It's important to understand the role of price guides in the antiques industry. The operative word is "guide." They're not intended to establish prices. That's why there's a disclaimer at the beginning of every one.

A Wave Crest perfume bottle might book at $350. You found one at a yard sale for only $10. Does this mean that your perfume bottle is worth $350? Not necessarily. It's only worth what your buyer is willing to pay.

Consider the variables. Does your clientele include anyone who is interested in perfume bottles? What kind of budget do those shoppers have? Are perfume bottles common or scarce in your area? More importantly, how often do you find examples of Wave Crest? Are you willing to price the bottle low enough that another dealer could buy it for resale? Or, are you going to price it close to book value and wait for the perfect buyer to come along?

Ultimately, it's you who will price that perfume bottle. Use price guides as just one of many factors in determining the bottle's value.

verify its maker. If you had provided a copy of *The Collectors Encyclopedia of Roseville Pottery* for him to look through, his uncertainty would have been erased when he found the item on page 66.

Customers will especially appreciate reference material if you specialize in a specific type of merchandise. A copy of *Early American Pattern Glass—1850 to 1910* would be a welcome addition to your display of pattern glass. Reference material is also appropriate when one of your displays focuses on a certain category of antiques and collectibles, such as cookie jars. A copy of *The Complete Cookie Jar Book* would enhance your display.

Reference material isn't limited to books. It can include newspaper and magazine clippings, catalog reprints, and even photocopies of pertinent material. Incorporate the information into your displays and highlight it. Include a shelf-talker telling customers the material is there for them to use. This suggests you want them to learn more about what you are selling.

Not everyone will use your reference material for the same purpose. Some who glance through your book on English porcelain might be interested in company histories, patterns, or sizes. Others might want to learn more about uses, reproductions, or values. Consider all the possibilities when deciding whether to include reference material with a display.

Most shoppers who use your reference material will be comparing prices. Current price guides are excellent reference books to put with a display because they encourage customers to check on your merchandise. If your prices are in line with the rest of the market, your customer will feel comfortable buying from you. If your prices are under book value, he will believe that he is getting a good deal.

33 Show That Items Work

IT PAYS TO STRUT YOUR STUFF.

Call it the rolltop-desk phenomenon. People love to watch things work. They'll slide the roll on a rolltop desk just to see it go up and down. They'll tinkle the keys of a piano just to hear it make noise. They'll wind a tin penguin toy just to watch it waddle. And, they'll peer through a telescope just to see what they can see. It's not that they expect to find Moby Dick peeking back at them; they're just curious.

This behavior is tolerated by most dealers, who sit and quietly frown as the rolling, tinkling, waddling, and peering is going on. However, as a dealer, all that activity should be telling you something. In addition to suggesting that humans are curious beasts, it tells you they need proof that the merchandise works.

There's no guarantee the customer winding your Chein penguin is simply curious. It's possible he actually wants to buy the piece, but only if it works properly. If that bird musters only two creaky steps, your customer probably won't give the purchase a second thought. But, if the penguin troops across the top of your showcase, your customer will eagerly pay cold cash to take it home.

Proving your merchandise works is not always as simple as moving the roll on a rolltop desk or peering through a telescope. Sometimes the customer needs assistance. He'll be more likely to buy your student lamp if it has a light bulb so he can test it. Likewise, he'll be more interested in your Fred Flintstone's Bedrock Band if you've provided batteries so he can watch Fred pound away at the drums.

You can turn on a potential customer by plugging in your electrical

When to Say When

There will actually be times when it's not a good idea for all your customers to see how an item works. You don't want every overzealous shopper who walks through your booth to play Ike Godsey with your National Cash Register, jabbing at the buttons and slamming the drawer. Sooner or later someone is going to poke one button too many, and that will be that. Your $800 cash register's number will be up. You can mark that sale "void."

What's a dealer to do? Use a shelf-talker to explain that the register is in good working condition. Include a polite message telling customers to ask for assistance if they'd like to further examine the item.

By placing batteries with this poodle toy, the dealer encourages interested shoppers to test his merchandise. A shelf-talker also informs the customer that the item is in good working condition.

items. Show him your Westinghouse brass-blade fan still creates quite a breeze. You'll have him dancing in the aisles when he knows your Wurlitzer jukebox still spins a tune.

Supply your customer with additional information about the merchandise, and he'll remember you long after his check clears the bank. Note that your Cat's Paw lighted advertising clock uses a 15-watt bulb, or employ a shelf-talker to emphasize the importance of placing a Seth Thomas mantel clock on a level surface. Your customer will appreciate knowing how to keep his purchase in working order.

▶ FYI

Go-withs to illustrate merchandise works:

1. Light bulbs in lights
2. Batteries in battery-operated toys
3. Keys with locks, clocks, and watches
4. Coins with mechanical banks
5. Paper in typewriters
6. Records on phonographs
7. Outlets near electric items

34 Decorate by Theme

SPRUCE UP OR SHIP OUT.

Time for a pop quiz. (Don't panic. It's multiple choice.) You're throwing a surprise birthday party for your father. How do you decorate the room?

a You don't

b Put up a Christmas tree and lights

c Hang a "Happy Birthday" banner and balloons

The correct answer, of course, is "c." Your decorations fit the theme of the party and create a festive atmosphere for the occasion. You can—and should—do the same in your shop or booth.

Using a theme to decorate your booth may increase sales. Decorations create a warm, welcoming atmosphere that puts your customers at ease. The better those customers feel about themselves and your merchandise, the more likely they are to make a purchase.

Patriotic decorations work well with this display of military-related merchandise. Props don't have to be elaborate to be effective. This display uses a stars-and-stripes banner, an American flag, and a "God bless America" shelf-talker.

Decorations also help distinguish your booth from others. Your booth will stand out if it is the only one that incorporates decorations in the overall scheme. Someone trying to remember where he saw the display of police badges might readily recall it was in the booth decorated for St. Patrick's Day.

You can use holidays to create decorative themes. Keep your decorations simple and incorporate everyday items into the displays. Tie an orange bow on a candlestick for Halloween or pin a sprig of holly on a doll at Christmas. Crystal that might otherwise be overlooked may be snapped up for Valentine's Day when paired with red glassware.

Holiday decorations should stay up for no more than a month. Some might only be needed for a week or two. It is particularly important to remove decorations immediately after the holiday. Optimally, your Halloween decorations should be taken down on November 1. Decorations that are out of season imply that you are lazy. If your Halloween decorations haven't been removed by the middle of November, customers will believe you haven't added any fresh merchandise in weeks.

Be creative. Decorations don't have to be holiday-related. They can also play off of special events, including sports. Display baseball pennants during the World Series or Olympic posters during The Games.

Also, consider the time of year and decorate by seasons. Hang a kite and pastel streamers as part of a spring theme. During summer months, use a wedding theme or highlight a local event, such as a county fair. Decorate with themes other dealers haven't considered, and your booth will stand out from all the rest.

When deciding what themes to use for decorating, consider your local population. A Hanukkah display might be appropriate in Brooklyn, but won't be as appreciated in Birmingham. Likewise, you wouldn't expect to

FYI

Non-holiday decorating themes:

1. Super Bowl Sunday
2. World Series
3. NBA playoffs
4. Stanley Cup
5. Indianapolis 500
6. Kentucky Derby
7. Olympics
8. Commemorative dates (moon landing)
9. Weddings (June)
10. Babies (August)
11. Local or state fairs and festivals
12. Seasons

see a hockey display in Florida, although it might be suitable in Minnesota or upstate New York.

Don't forget that you can also decorate by color. The customer trying to remember where he saw the grain-painted dough box will readily recall it was in the slate-blue booth.

How much should you decorate? There are no guidelines. Use enough decorations that your theme is understood, but don't overdo it. Your goal is to emphasize your merchandise, not overpower it. If your shoppers are overwhelmed by your decorating scheme, they may overlook your merchandise. Rather than seeing your Buddy-L truck and Lionel train set at the base of your Christmas tree, they'll spend their time gazing at the ornaments and flashing lights. Strive to achieve a visual balance between merchandise and decorative elements.

35 Promote Gifts

FUN WITH DICK AND JANE.

Jane's birthday is Saturday. You don't know Jane. Nor do you know her husband, Dick. But Dick will be walking into your shop any time now. You'll recognize him by the frown on his face and the way he scratches his head. Dick doesn't have the slightest idea what to buy Jane.

The moment Dick enters your shop, his problem becomes your problem. It doesn't matter that you don't know Dick or Jane. What's important is that your role just changed—from merchant to problem-solver. Dick needs help, and you are in a position to lend a hand.

You can provide assistance in several ways. Take an active role in helping Dick spot an appropriate birthday present for his wife. Ask him questions about Jane and get a general idea of her likes and dislikes. Make some suggestions and show possible choices to Dick.

Sometimes assistance isn't this straightforward, however. Dick might

This display of baby-related items uses a shelf-talker to promote the merchandise as non-traditional shower gifts. The shelf-talker reads, "Everyone loves a baby. Whole collections are based on baby-related items, from tiny shoes to decorated talc tins. Baby-related collectibles also make great non-traditional shower gifts."

> **FYI**
>
> Gift-giving occasions that can be used to promote merchandise:
>
> 1. Holidays
> 2. Birthdays
> 3. Weddings
> 4. Anniversaries
> 5. Baby showers
> 6. Baptisms, christenings
> 7. First communion, confirmation
> 8. Graduations
> 9. Housewarmings
> 10. Just for the fun of it

not share his problem with you. He might be so intent on his task that he walks right past you, barely mumbling hello as he shuffles his way to the sales floor. This man on a mission is going it alone. When you ask if you can help him find anything, he'll shake his head and just keep looking. Now it's up to your merchandise to sell itself. If you've planned ahead, this is not a problem.

Use creative displays to remind your customer that antiques are wonderful gifts. Catch Dick's eye with a birthday display. Highlight the display by incorporating balloons, bows, and party hats. Add a shelf-talker to emphasize the promotion.

Other gift-giving occasions can also be used to help sell your merchandise. In June, promote silver and fine glassware as wedding presents. Group together crib quilts, rocking chairs, and Bessie Pease Gutmann prints as presents for a baby shower. Of course, don't forget holidays such as Christmas and Valentine's Day.

Keep in mind that gifts aren't just for grandmothers anymore. Be innovative. Promote gifts for the baby sitter, paperboy, or car pool driver—people your customer might not normally consider buying antiques for. Your costume jewelry, Case pocketknife, or felt Buick pennant might do the trick. Keep these items relatively inexpensive, though. Your customer may want to buy a small gift for his mail carrier, but he probably won't want to spend much to do so.

36 Have Items Ready to Go

MAKE YOURS A ONE-STOP ANTIQUE SHOP.

It's a jungle out there, beyond the friendly confines of your antique shop. Inside your shop it's warm and inviting. Inside your shop there are treasures galore. Inside your shop the customer clutches a precious find to his chest. Often, that piece is a gift: the *perfect* item for the person who has everything. Your customer is smiling as he carries his purchase toward the door. He steps outside. And then depression sets in.

He still has to find a box for the darned thing.

Off he trudges, through the cold and the snow and the muck, in search of a box. And paper. And a bow. Some way to make his gift pretty. If only you could have helped him. The trouble is, you could have.

You can encourage sales by following an approach long-used by traditional retailers—have gift items ready to go. Traditional retailers generally carry duplicate merchandise and can interest the last-minute shopper by wrapping items ahead of time. When the customer chooses the boxed candy he wants to give his sweetie as a Valentine's Day present, the clerk reaches under the counter and pulls out a pre-wrapped box. Instant gift.

However, it's not likely you'll have a dozen identical Parker Lucky Curve pens—one on display and eleven gift wrapped. With the right approach, however, you can still promote your one pen as a gift. Provide a

Improve your customer service by providing special bags and boxes for gift purchases. A shelf-talker emphasizes that a gift bag is available with this Cat in the Hat alarm clock.

It's in the Bag

Where are you going to find special containers to hold gift merchandise? Check the Yellow Pages under "bags" and "boxes." A variety of companies sell all kinds and sizes.

However, don't overlook the more creative approach. Handmade boxes and bags emphasize the unique characteristics of your merchandise. The owner of one antique mall stencils holiday symbols on plain paper sacks.

If you don't have the time or artistic talent, involve others in your project. Work with students at local elementary schools or residents of a nearby nursing home to create your gift boxes and bags. The result may be a piece of modern-day folk art your customers are bound to remember.

small gift box or bag. Or, dress it up with a ribbon or bow. This works particularly well for large merchandise. Place a ribbon and bow on your oak sleigh bed or around your Simon and Halbig doll, and the customer won't fret over wrapping it.

This technique is especially effective during holidays, when gift buying increases. Cater to the last-minute shopper. A bag with a Christmas theme might be perfect for packaging an unwieldy German feather tree. Stock several sizes of gift boxes to hold everything from a sterling silver thimble to a Battenburg tablecloth.

Regardless of the approach you use, your goal is to offer one-stop shopping. Merchandise that is gift-ready may encourage customers to buy from you rather than a store down the street.

Don't despair over the expense of buying special boxes, bags, and ribbons. The initial cost will be more than offset by the goodwill this service creates.

37 Offer Extras: Information, Services, and Supplies

GO ABOVE AND BEYOND THE CALL OF DUTY.

If John F. Kennedy had gone into sales rather than politics, he probably would have said, "And so, my fellow retailers, ask not what your customers can do for you; ask what you can do for your customers."

Consumers rely on you for more than just merchandise. They look to you for information. They depend on you to answer their questions, whether they want to know who can appraise grandma's silver tea service or where they can get a set of chairs caned. Dealers who can provide the answers are appreciated and remembered.

One shopper might want to know when the Fostoria Glass Co. was founded. You could quickly check a general price guide and report that Fostoria was established in 1887. Another customer might ask about other antique shops in your area. You can tell him about the mall in town and also direct him to a rack of brochures for other area shops.

Some questions may have absolutely nothing to do with antiques and collectibles, but they are still important to your customer. If he asks where the nearest automated teller machine is located, be sure you know. It may be your Rotary Iced Tea cooler he'll have to forgo if he can't come up with the cash.

When you don't know the answer to a customer's question, admit it. However, you should still make an effort to find the answer. When necessary, refer customers to others who can provide the information. You might not know the best way to clean a horsehair sofa, but the shop owner next door may have the answer. Refer the customer to the other dealer.

Your customer will also turn to you for help with special problems. He might need an Elgin pocket watch repaired or a dresser mirror resilvered.

Tip Your Customer

One mall dealer uses a "Tip of the Week" to generate customer interest. Each tip provides information the customer might find useful. "Add vinegar to water to make glass sparkle." Or, "Never wrap flatware with a rubber band. The rubber will tarnish the silver." These tips are neatly lettered on a small piece of poster board prominently displayed in the booth. A similar approach may work well for you.

One for the Road

Most shops and malls use special racks to highlight an assortment of fliers from other antique shops. These brochures are especially helpful for customers who are traveling and may be unfamiliar with the area.

You can further assist these shoppers by dividing that rack into sections labeled north, south, east, and west. File the brochures according to the location of the shop or mall. If Greeley's Antiques Emporium is west of your mall, file their fliers under that heading. A shopper searching for Greeley's place won't need anyone to tell him, "Go west, young man."

For the customer, this eliminates the hassle of scrounging through a table of fliers to find ones for shops along his travel route. If he is traveling north, he can look under the appropriate heading and choose brochures.

You might also want to borrow an interstate rest-area technique. Enhance the display with an area or state map and use color-coded map pins to note the location of other shops and malls.

Fliers for area antique shops and malls can be organized by compass direction. A shopper heading south only needs to look for material on the appropriate row. The sign accompanying the map states, "Map pins indicate sites of other antique shops and malls."

You can help him by either providing the service or referring him to someone who does.

Use signs or shelf-talkers to promote the services you offer. Tell the customer you provide free furniture delivery within a fifty-mile radius. Describe your layaway policy. Note which of the major credit cards you accept.

You can also help your customers by selling supplies and reference materials. Supplies can include restoration hardware, furniture cleaners and waxes, and refinishing products. Reference materials can include price guides and trade papers.

Regardless of whether your customer is seeking information, supplies, or services, your goal is to provide him with excellent customer service. Customers who receive personalized service will reward those businesses with their loyalty.

38 Consider the Environmental Sensitivity Factor

SOOTHE THE SAVAGE SENSES.

You know the saying, "Beauty is in the eye of the beholder." What one person sees as beautiful may be your text-book definition of ugly. In your case, the "beholder" is the customer. He may be affected by his physical surroundings in a different way than you are. What he hears, feels, sees, and smells can promote or inhibit buying.

Smell, in particular, is an important factor in determining one's mood, and customers can be turned away if they find an odor offensive or overwhelming. Keep in mind, what's unobtrusive to you may be unbearable to your customers. Ask anyone who's visiting a pig farm. Farmer McDonald might not mind the aroma. He's so used to it, he doesn't even notice. But, a guest is likely to wrinkle his nose in disgust.

If you sell potpourri, scented candles, or soaps, make sure the scent is not overpowering. Some customers may be particularly sensitive to certain smells. Others may have allergies which can be triggered by substances in your booth, including dust.

Likewise, some people find cigarette or cigar smoke particularly annoying. They may avoid your booth if you or another customer is smoking.

Even pay attention to your bathrooms. How do they smell? Are they noticeable down the hall? An unclean or stinky bathroom can put customers in a foul mood.

What your customer hears can also have a negative impact. This is especially true of background music. You might like heavy metal, but it's probably not appropriate for your shop. Metallica or Poison don't set the mood for buying Belleek tea cups or a Hepplewhite candle stand. Music that is loud or fast can make shoppers feel antsy and want to leave. Music that is slow or hypnotic may put them to sleep. Instead, choose music that appeals to a broad range of customers and that helps put them at ease.

Some malls use a public address system to tell their customers about specific policies, such as layaways, or to notify them when the mall is about to close for the day. Although these announcements can be helpful, they need to be done in a professional manner. If the individual making the announcement sounds bored or uses poor grammar, customers are likely to be annoyed rather than appreciative.

Lighting can also affect your customer's buying moods. Poor lighting makes it difficult to see what is on display, while overly bright lights or those at eye level can be irritating if not blinding. Whether you're using

He Should Have Tried the Decaf

The sensitivity factor can also include physical responses, such as pain. The customer who cracks his skull on a cast-iron kettle hanging from a rafter may spend more time rubbing his head than looking at your merchandise (not to mention the time he'll spend consulting his attorney). Accidents will happen, but you can decrease their likelihood. Use a little common sense when arranging your merchandise. Remember, hurting customers aren't good buyers.

The same is true of embarrassed or angry shoppers. In one mall, a customer was interested in a contemporary stoneware coffee cup. What he didn't know was that the cup, which was half full, had been left in the booth by the dealer. When the shopper turned the cup over to check for a mark, he dumped coffee on himself, a schoolmaster's desk, and the floor. Flustered and still dripping, he went to the front desk to ask for assistance. The mall employee seemed more bothered than concerned. Needless to say, the customer got mad and quickly left without making a purchase.

ceiling lights, track lighting, or clip-on lamps, be sure they illuminate the merchandise without distracting the customer.

The sensitivity factor can also include emotional and psychological responses to your merchandise. Some items may strike a positive note with shoppers. A customer might buy your Yard of Kittens print because it's identical to the one that hung in his grandmother's living room. However, be aware that merchandise can also put a customer in a negative frame of mind. Your American Legion graveside flag holder will be considered inappropriate if he thinks it belongs next to a veteran's tombstone, not in an antique shop. That could be enough to make him boycott everything in your booth.

39 Establish Ties with Local Merchants

BE A TEAM PLAYER.

Aisle 1: Produce. You're minding your own business, choosing bananas. When what to your wondering eyes appear? Antiques. In a supermarket?

That's what shoppers found when they pushed their carts down the produce aisle of one grocery store. The store manager had asked a local antique mall for assistance in creating a display to promote peaches. The mall owner supplied measuring cups, mixing bowls, pie pans, a rolling pin, and an enamel cook stove for a display extolling homemade pies. An accompanying sign noted that the props were on loan from the mall. Both merchants profited from the display. The store sold a few more peaches, and the antique mall got some free publicity.

You can call attention to your shop or mall by teaming up with businesses in your community. Talk to local merchants about using some of your merchandise as props in their displays. You might exhibit a Singer treadle sewing machine, patterns, and a vintage gown in a local fabric store. Or, you could display a scale, bitters bottles, and a nineteenth-century druggist sign in a pharmacy. A sign and fliers with the display will explain your involvement.

Bookstores provide excellent opportunities for using this display technique. You might include a small selection of Northwood's Grape & Cable with the store's display of a new Carnival glass book. In turn, set up a similar display in your shop and add a shelf-talker telling customers where they can purchase the book. You'll be increasing product awareness at the same time you're generating customer interest.

Smaller, privately owned businesses are often more willing to work your merchandise into a display. Many chain stores must follow company

Make a Close Call

To find additional businesses to approach about setting up special displays, "Let your fingers do the walking." Check the Yellow Pages.

Look at the major headings to see what types of businesses are in your area. You'll probably come up with locations you had overlooked. A hobby shop could be the perfect place to display your vintage train sets, or the telephone company might be interested in an exhibit of early communication equipment.

Public libraries are particulary good locations for displaying antiques and collectibles. A book on almost any topic can be paired with related merchandise. This display features radios of the 1920s. (Display from New Castle-Henry County Public Library, New Castle, Indiana)

policies requiring approval from corporate headquarters before setting up displays. You may still be able to work with these businesses, but allow additional time for the necessary paperwork and approval.

These multi-retailer displays do not always have to mirror the nature of the particular business you are working with. Libraries often provide a special area for thematic displays. Some banks promote community awareness and pride by asking different area merchants to set up displays on a monthly basis. Don't assume that your library will only be interested in a display of early books or that a bank will only consider a display of nineteenth-century coins.

▶ FYI

Ideas for creative promotional displays:

1. Athletic store—sports equipment
2. Automobile dealership—advertising, toy or model cars
3. Bakery—aprons, utensils, cookbooks
4. Bank—toy banks, currency
5. Book store—any subject related to a specific book
6. Camera shop—vintage cameras, equipment, photographs
7. Clothing store—vintage clothing, seasonal items
8. Electric company—early electric appliances
9. Fabric shop—sewing machine, patterns, vintage clothing
10. Fitness center—athletic equipment, sports photos
11. Florist shop—vases, small room setting
12. Hardware store—tools
13. Hobby shop—trains or models
14. Jewelry store—vintage jewelry
15. Library—any subject suitable for readers
16. Music store—musical instruments, sheet music
17. Optometrist—eye glasses, optometric charts
18. Pharmacy—early drug store items
19. Telephone company—vintage telephones
20. Video rental shop—items related to new releases

V Effective Price Tags

Price tag etiquette. You won't hear about it from Miss Manners, but it does exist. Pricing your merchandise involves more than scribbling numbers on a tag and slapping it on the item. What your tags look like and how you use them can affect your customer's purchasing decisions.

Confusing or illegible price tags can hinder sales. A customer may walk away from your hand-carved cane if an indecipherable price is the only information on the tag. If your tag had noted the cane was made by a well-known woodcarver, and if the price had been easy to read, you might not have lost the sale.

Your merchandise will determine which type of price tag you use. Logically, your cameo ring would require a different kind of tag than your walnut secretary. Sale merchandise also needs special tags. For instance, a bright-orange price tag will deliver a knock-out punch when you place your Popeye Strength Tester on sale.

Regardless of the type of tag you use, if it damages the merchandise, you're going to lose the sale. A customer who is considering purchasing your "High Noon" poster will shoot down the idea when he sees your adhesive sticker is stuck to it.

40 Use Nonabusive Tags

PRUDENT PLACEMENT PREVENTS STICKER SHOCK.

What's wrong with this picture? A dealer has a 1930s Mobiloil poster for sale. He thoughtfully places the price tag on a Post-It Note, which he then puts on the poster. He's concerned that the tag not damage the paper. So far, so good. Then he securely tapes the poster to the wall.

Ugh!

The dealer's actions are a perfect example of a good idea turned bad. Really bad. He is to be commended for using a Post-It Note with the price tag. But, there was a lapse in the thought process—it was counterproductive to tape the poster to the wall. That's as harmful as a carelessly placed price tag.

Collectors and dealers are increasingly particular about the condition of the merchandise they buy. They are more discriminating and less likely to purchase flawed items. Who can blame them? No one wants damaged goods. What's so disconcerting, however, is that often a piece will be needlessly damaged by its own price tag.

Adhesive price tags are the worst offenders. When removed, they can pull paint off your toleware spice box, damage the patina on your mahogany sideboard, or even discolor the cover on your first edition of T.S. Eliot's *Ash Wednesday*.

The most common mistake unthinking dealers make is to place adhesive stickers on paper items. Price tags are stuck on magazine covers, the flyleaves of books, cardboard advertising boxes, and photographs. Often, the stickers can't be removed without damaging the item. Your customer may not even consider buying your Beatles calendar if he doubts he can safely remove the price tag. And placing the sticker on the back of the piece

FYI

Potentially harmful pricing methods:

1. Adhesive tags can tear paper, discolor fabric, damage paint and patina.
2. Paper clips can scratch merchandise and leave rust stains.
3. Lock tags—don't get them so tight they can't be safely cut off.
4. Safety pins and straight pins can damage delicate fabrics and leave rust stains.
5. Pens may leave permanent marks.
6. Pencil marks, even light erasing can damage merchandise.

or on the inside is not an acceptable alternative. Although the damage caused by removing the price tag may not be immediately and readily visible, it is still damage, nonetheless.

Nonabusive pricing methods preserve the integrity of your merchandise and demonstrate its value. Customers will be more likely to buy from you when they know you make a conscious effort to keep your merchandise in the best condition possible.

Post-It Notes are one substitute for adhesive price tags. The original adhesive tag can be stuck to the Post-It Note, which can then be placed on the merchandise. The note can be harmlessly removed and reapplied.

If you use Post-It Notes, remember to check them frequently. Over time, the adhesive can weaken or become dirty, causing the tag to fall off.

String tags and lock tags are other nonabusive pricing methods. Because these tags do not adhere to the merchandise, they present no risk of damaging the item. Lock tags are often preferred, however, because they deter price-tag switching. Loop one through the handle of your Cowden & Wilcox jug or around the neck of your G.I. Joe doll. There will be no doubt the tags go with those items.

Five types of nonabusive tags are shown here. A shelf-talker is used with the battery-operated train, a string tag with the papier mâché Santa, a Post-It Note with the Superman card, a lock tag with the Monarch bottle, and a table tent with the Mighty Mouse squeeze toy.

Time Is Against You

Keep in mind that even "safe" methods of pricing your merchandise can be harmful over time. Acids in your tags may discolor merchandise. Likewise, exposure to sunlight may cause the item to fade, leaving a darker area where the tag was located. Make sure merchandise does not stay in direct sunlight for a prolonged period.

Don't wait for a problem to develop. If you're unsure of the long-range effects of a particular type of tag, use an alternative.

Shelf-talkers can also be used to show an item's price. Make sure the price is prominent and there is no confusion over which item the shelf-talker accompanies. Add the price to the bottom of your shelf-talker explaining the historic significance of your Chicago Daily Tribune's "Dewey Defeats Truman" issue.

Give special consideration to how you price items in locked showcases. Customers must be able to see both the item and its price tag. This can be quite a challenge when the item is small. How many times have you seen a showcase of jewelry and had no idea how much the pieces were priced? If the tag isn't visible, your customer might not take the time to have you open the case.

Partially obstructed tags can be equally troublesome. It may be that the price is covered enough to make it questionable. If all the customer can see is a "5", he's really left in the dark. Is the Art Nouveau hat pin priced five dollars, fifty-something or something-five?

Special string tags for jewelry are helpful for pricing small items in a showcase. Post-It Notes can also be used, placed on the shelf directly in

A Sticky Situation

What do you do when you buy someone else's mistake—an item that may be damaged when you remove the adhesive price tag? Remove the tag with lighter fluid.

Rubber cement is the adhesive compound on most price tags, and it can be dissolved by a number of solutions, including lighter fluid. If possible, test for staining by applying lighter fluid to an inconspicuous area first.

Then, soak the tag and be patient. When the adhesive dissolves, the tag can be peeled from the item.

Adhesive price tags can damage many antiques and collectibles. This Coca-Cola blotter was ruined when the sticker was removed.

front of the item. Or, table tents can be set next to the merchandise. Regardless of the method used, make sure it is obvious which items the tags go with.

Some items aren't amenable to attaching price tags. Be creative when necessary. Your child's blanket might pose a special problem. An adhesive tag is likely to fall off. And, there's no hole for attaching a string tag or lock tag. The solution—use a safety pin. Attach the pin to the blanket, then loop a string or lock tag through the pin.

41 Change Your Price Tags

YOU NEVER KNOW WHEN THEY'LL HAVE AN ACCIDENT.

Politicians will tell you, it's time for a change. A change in leadership. A change in policies. A change in taxes. A change in price tags. Price tags?

Well, not exactly. Politicians couldn't care less, but customers do.

Dirty or faded price tags suggest that your merchandise has been displayed for an extended period of time. A dirty tag on your cheese mold or a faded tag on your Heisey vase tells the customer no one else is interested in the piece. Even though there may be nothing wrong with the item, a worn tag raises all kinds of questions. Is the piece damaged? Is the price too high? Why has it been here so long? In short, the customer sees the tag and assumes the merchandise is not saleable.

Periodically check the price tags on your merchandise to ensure they are in good shape. If any are torn or damaged, replace them. Pay particular attention to tags on merchandise located in window areas, where they may fade to the point where they literally cannot be read. Your goal is to create the impression your merchandise is fresh: new tags should do the trick.

Replace price tags that look this bad. The tag on the stoneware jar is smeared and difficult to read.

▶ FYI

Change your price tags when:

1. They are dirty
2. They are damaged
3. They lose their adhesiveness
4. The ink is faded
5. The ink is smeared
6. You take mall merchandise to a show
7. You lower the price

The crumpled Post-It Note on this vintage photograph suggests the item has been on sale for a prolonged period. A new tag will suggest that this is a fresh piece of merchandise.

Smeared tags also present a negative image. Your R.S. Suhl compote won't seem so glamorous if the price tag looks like it's been through the rinse cycle a time or two. You might have accidentally smudged the ink when you wrote the tag, or a customer with sweaty hands might have smeared the ink while handling the piece. In either case, the tag should be replaced.

If the tag on your Jim Beam caboose bottle keeps falling off, it's trying to tell you something. Likewise, the tag on your mahogany game table will

Beware the Man with a Pen

Some dealers are slashers and scribblers. When an item doesn't sell, they slash through the old price and scribble in a new one. To add to the confusion, they often initial the change.

There's a better way to re-price your merchandise.

When you lower the price, make a new tag. The slash-and-scribble method broadcasts that the item has been in your shop for an extended period. A new tag makes the merchandise look fresh. Customers who have not previously seen your amberina bride's basket will not know that it has been in your shop for nine months. The basket will have more appeal when your customer believes it is a new addition.

If you want to place that basket on sale, use a special sale tag that clearly indicates the price has been lowered. Make sure the customer knows what the piece was initially priced. Note the original price on the sale tag or leave the regular tag on the basket. Rewrite that original tag if it is dirty, faded, or damaged.

look unprofessional if the corners are peeling. Replace your price tags when they begin to lose their adhesiveness.

Price tags don't have to lose their adhesiveness to look tacky. Mall tags may look out of place when used on merchandise at shows. Shoppers are accustomed to mall tags that indicate your booth number. This is necessary at an antique mall. However, these same tags convey an altogether different impression at shows. Show-goers want to feel they are seeing fresh merchandise, not items you couldn't sell at your mall. When they see mall tags on merchandise, they may think you simply pulled merchandise from your booth and placed it in the show. They'll ask themselves, "If it didn't sell at a mall, why should I buy it here?" Take the extra time to switch tags.

42 Use Special Tags for Sale Merchandise

IT'S TIME FOR SHOW AND SELL.

Shoppers love sales. They thrive on bargains. Some people will spend an entire day driving the tires off their car just to find the best buys, whether they are saving a few dollars on groceries or purchasing back-to-school clothes for their children.

Sale merchandise will also turn heads in your shop. Use highly visible sale tags that emphasize the reduced price. Sale tags that are a different style and color will stand out. They make it obvious that your Mills slot machine is on sale or that the price has been lowered on your Geisha Girl porcelain.

Traditionally, orange tags signify sale merchandise, but any vibrant color can be used. The one exception is red, which is generally reserved for sold tags. If you use a red tag to discount your Uhl polar bear jug, your customer might not realize it's on sale. He may assume the piece has been sold and walk by without giving it a second look.

It is extremely important that you show the original price and the sale price so your customer can make an informed decision. Let him know he is getting a bargain. If the tag on your innkeeper's trade sign shows only the $275 sale price, he might think the item is rather expensive. However, if he sees that the price has been reduced from $475, the sign might seem like a steal. When he's hanging it in his family room, he'll even brag to his wife about the great deal he got.

Never (as in NEVER!) inflate an item's original price to make its sale price seem particularly appealing. Customers have good memories. They'll recall that your Godzilla model was priced $80 last month, but now the tag shows $120 as the original price and $80 as the sale price. Your lack of principles might help sell the model to an unsuspecting shopper, but it may also ruin your reputation with long-standing customers.

The Color of Success

Although orange price tags can be used to emphasize sale merchandise, they can also promote non-sale merchandise. Several companies use this technique. One company places orange price tags on its snack food packages. A national chain of toy stores also uses orange tags on all its merchandise. Some customers see the orange tags and buy the items, assuming they are on sale. Keep in mind, however, that some people consider this practice unethical.

They Think What They Want

Dealers acquire their merchandise for little or nothing. They find it on street corners, take advantage of uninformed sellers, or trick elderly owners.

Of course, this is seldom the case. Yet, many people have a negative impression of antiques dealers and incorrectly assume the worst. These are the people who scoff at the need for sales in the antiques industry. They know most dealers already give discounts of one sort or another to a large portion of their clientele, and a sale sends off warning signals. "If this dealer can give discounts *and* have sales, the prices must be too high," the customer thinks. He sees a sale as proof that the dealer is making a huge profit on what he sells.

If you do hold a sale, it should be limited in scope. Booth-wide clearances create the impression you are going out of business. Try to avoid them. Instead, focus on items that have been in stock too long or that you no longer wish to carry.

Of course, you don't have to have sales at all.

One myth in the antiques industry is that it's important to always have a sale of some kind. Reduced-price sales can be dangerous. They result in a quick rush of increased business, which can become addictive. A dealer

A variety of effective sale tags are available. A large, yellow-and-red string tag shows the regular price and the discount price of the lumberjack whirligig. An orange, sunburst "Special" sticker is used on the covered stoneware jar. The souvenir plate is priced with a square, yellow-and-red "Sale" sticker, and the high-top shoes carry a large, yelllow-and-red "Sale Price" string tag.

What If You Held a Sale and Nobody Bought?

There's definitely a wrong way to have a sale. The "Dutch" sale, in which an item is reduced by a set amount over pre-determined intervals, is an excellent example of what not to do.

It works this way. Your $275 walnut church pew has been gathering dust in your shop for months. You decide to put it on sale. But this isn't just any sale. This is a special sale. You make a sign showing the original price and the reduced price, $250. Your sign notes that the price will be lowered by $25 every week until the pew is sold.

Then you wait. A week passes. Two weeks. Three weeks. Each Monday you slash through the old price and write in a new one. $225. $200. $175. Your sign resembles a score card from a bowling tournament. Numbers everywhere. Another week, another $25. Unfortunately, you've discovered the perfect way to emphasize that no one wants to buy the pew.

This method may even encourage customers not to buy your merchandise. A shopper who likes your pew may gamble that it will still be available in two weeks, when it will be $50 cheaper. Your sale actually gives him a reason to walk away without making the purchase.

may resort to sales to keep the cash register ringing. Eventually, those sales can be counter-productive. Frequent sales can cause regular customers to hesitate when considering a purchase. Instead of buying your copper coffee server for the $300 asking price, your customer might gamble that it will go on sale. The longer he waits, the greater the chance he might lose interest in the piece.

Sales tend to appeal to those people who concentrate on the cheapest goods and shy away from the most profitable merchandise. This can create an unhealthy customer base. People who patronize a business simply because of its sales are not likely to be steady customers. Instead, they are a fickle lot who go where the prices are lowest.

You don't have to steer away from sales completely, but don't depend on them. If you can build your business without ever having a sale, then do. Your customers may be more loyal, and their word-of-mouth referrals will be based on more than just reduced prices.

43 Consider Tag Placement and Visibility

"IT'S NOT PRICED. MUST BE FREE."

You'd like to sell your cherry-red 1957 Corvette. You lovingly wash and wax it. You proudly display it in your front yard. You put the "For Sale" sign where?

a Under the driver's-side floor mat
b In the house on the kitchen table
c In the car's front window

Of course, you place the "For Sale" sign in the front window of the automobile. That's only logical. You want passers-by to know that your car is for sale, not think it's under the tree just for the shade.

You need to adopt the same logical approach when placing price tags on your merchandise. Items will sell more readily if the tags are both accessible and visible. Only the most serious or curious of customers will take the time to search for an out-of-sight price tag.

Make shopping as easy as possible for your customers. One dealer tagged his 3-gallon stoneware churn on the side opposite the cobalt decoration. When the piece was displayed so the price could be seen, the decoration was not visible. The dealer could have taken advantage of the unique feature of the churn by placing the tag next to the cobalt decoration, where both could be readily noted.

Another dealer placed the price tag on the bottom of an umbrella stand—on the inside! Obviously, the tag was nearly impossible to find. Not

Two Tags Aren't Better than One

Double check all of your merchandise before you put it on display. Make sure you take the price tags off items you buy to resell.

Did you remove the price tag from the McCoy cookie jar you bought at a yard sale last week? If not, a customer is going to want to pay the $5 price on the yard sale tag, not the $65 price on your tag. Likewise, make sure you remove your original tag if you change the regular price of an item. The shopper will be confused if one tag on your primitive wheelbarrow says $225 and another says $175.

When a discrepancy occurs, honor the lower price. You might lose $60 by selling your McCoy cookie jar for the yard sale price, but you'll most certainly lose that customer's future business if you tell him he has to pay the higher amount. He won't listen to your excuse. All he'll hear is that he can't have the item for what it's marked. Take the loss and keep the customer.

The Case of the Missing Price Tags

The story you are about to read is true. The merchandise has been changed to protect the innocent.

10:28 a.m. A tall, slender officer knocks at the door. The perfect man for the job. He's quick. He's cunning. He's crafty. He's at the wrong address.

10:36 a.m. Having circled the block three times, he finally arrives at the scene. He parks his car and double checks the mailbox. Right place. He straightens his tie and heads for the door. He's on a mission. An impossible mission: find the price tag.

10:37 a.m. He enters the shop and flashes his badge. "Mrs. Bates? I'm Detective Bass, Antiques Police. We've received an anonymous tip concerning your shop. I have a warrant. I need to have a look at your tags."

10:38 a.m. He begins his investigation. Mrs. Bates watches fearfully.

"Ah, the evidence shows there's been no recent activity in this area," Bass says. "None of these prints have been touched in months. Mrs. Bates, do your customers even know they are for sale?"

"Of course they do," she snaps. "They all have price tags. Even a simpleton knows to take them off the wall and look on the back. Don't try to pin this one on me!"

Bass flips open a small notebook and scribbles something. "Take it easy, Ma'am. I'm just doing my job," he responds. "Could you unlock that showcase, please? Gotta be thorough."

"There's really no need," she responds gruffly, pulling the keys from her pocket.

10:45 a.m. Bass continues his investigation. "Just as I thought," he says. "All these items are priced on the bottom. It would take a psychic to read these tags." More scribbles.

"What's it matter?" she retorts. "If they're real interested, they'll ask."

10:49 a.m. Bass kneels by a twenty-gallon crock and continues his search. He examines the outside. He examines the inside. He scratches his head. He strains to turn the piece over. At last, he finds the tag—taped to the bottom. "What is the meaning of this?" he asks. "How could anyone find this tag?"

"You found it, didn't you?" she growls.

"This isn't looking good, Ma'am," he says. "Not good at all." He stands and looks at a quilt hanging from the ceiling. "Nope, not good at all," he mumbles, searching for the price tag. "I'll need a chair or a stool, please."

10:55 a.m. Grudgingly, Mrs. Bates complies. The detective climbs on the chair, craning his neck to see the tag pinned to the upper-right corner. More scribbles in the notebook.

Out of the corner of his eye, Detective Bass catches Mrs. Bates sliding something into a desk drawer. He quickly unsnaps his holster. "Step away from that desk. Now!" he demands. She drops her head and does as ordered.

10:58 a.m. Bass hurries to the desk, opens the drawer, and shakes his head. "Ma'am, I've seen plenty of cases of merchandise abuse, but this is by far the worst." He empties the drawer onto the desk. Paper items. All with tags—adhesive tags—stuck to the front. Postcards. Railroad timetables. Calendars. Blotters. "You've ruined every one of these items. This is a sad day, indeed."

11:04 a.m. Bass reaches for his handcuffs. "I'll have to take you to the station, Ma'am. You have the right to remain silent . . ."

Another day. Another case solved. Another triumph for the Antiques Police.

Mrs. Bates was tried and convicted in circuit court on forty-nine counts of Improper Tag Placement. She is currently making license plates at the federal correctional institution in Lompoc, California.

only was it in a highly unusual location, but it was also buried beneath candy wrappers and empty pop cans. Both the tag placement and the accumulated trash suggested that the dealer wasn't really concerned about either his merchandise or his customers.

Remember, the more people you interest in your merchandise, the greater your chance of making a sale. A casual shopper might think your stained glass window is beautiful, but he'll probably not give any real consideration to buying it if he can't readily determine the price. However, that window might have been a bargain, and you could have sold it, had he found the hidden price tag that told him it was within his budget. Make sure price tages are visible. Impatient shoppers will walk away from items that seem to be unpriced.

Ensuring a tag's visibility requires more effort than just slapping it on anywhere. Know where every tag should optimally be located on each item.

Price tags are of little use when they can't be seen. When these smalls are locked in a showcase, the customer won't be able to access the tags without seeking assistance. Using the same merchandise, these photos illustrate effective and ineffective use of price tags. One shows price tags that can't be read or that cover the merchandise, and the other demonstrates improved tag usage.

Devise a uniform system of tag placement. Consistency is important. For instance, all your framed prints might be tagged in the upper-right corner. You will confuse your customers if one print is tagged in the upper-right corner, another in the lower-left corner, and a third on the back.

Likewise, it doesn't make sense to tag one chair on a bottom rung, a second on a back spindle, and another on an arm. This is confusing. Don't make the customer do any more work than is necessary. Help him to know where to look by putting tags in the same general area on similar pieces of merchandise.

Accessibility is also important. Can your shoppers reach every tag? Keep in mind those customers with physical disabilities. A person with a bad back might not be able to reach the tag on the bottom rung of a chair, yet some dealers have priced chairs in that fashion. Likewise, someone in a wheelchair will have a hard time reading a price tag at the top of an oak highboy.

Give special consideration to price tag placement on merchandise inside locked showcases. If the tag is beneath your English straight razor, it's impossible for the customer to see the price. Instead, he has to find someone to unlock the case and remove the razor before he even knows if it's in his price range. Few shoppers will go to the trouble.

Check the items in your showcases on a frequent basis. Are the price tags clearly visible? When necessary, use jewelry tags, Post-It Notes, table tents, or shelf-talkers. Make sure all the tags are face up and not obscured by the merchandise. Even if your $20 gold piece is marked "free," you won't give it away if the tag isn't visible.

Remember, proper price tag placement is a priority for all your merchandise, not just the more expensive pieces. Your $2 Bustlin' Betsy Swanky Swig should be priced with the same care as your $20,000 T.C. Steele landscape.

44 Write Legibly

BMALE LT TILA $S DAHYR AM.

Have you ever looked at a price tag and felt you'd have a better chance deciphering ancient Egyptian hieroglyphics? You're not sure if the figures you see are the price, the booth number, or the dealer's shoe size. To make matters worse, you can't decipher the description. "Quaker Oatmeal" or "Don Ho's Ukulele." Who can tell?

Penmanship is important. When a price tag is illegible, the resulting confusion can stifle a sale. Customers who can easily read and understand your tags are more likely to reward you with a purchase.

Human nature dictates that your customer probably won't ask about a confusing price tag, especially if he has to leave your booth and walk to the front of the mall to find someone who might not know anyway. Make the customer's task as simple as possible. Present the information on your tags in a neat and orderly fashion that can be easily understood.

The clearest component of any tag should be the price. Make it the dominant item and separate it from the rest of the information. Be consistent from tag to tag and keep things as simple as possible. When an item is priced an even-dollar amount, there's no need to use double zeros for cents. The extra numbers only clutter the tag. Undoubtedly, at least one shopper will wonder if your Little Orphan Annie decoder is priced $25.00 or $2500. Avoid confusion by simply pricing the decoder $25.

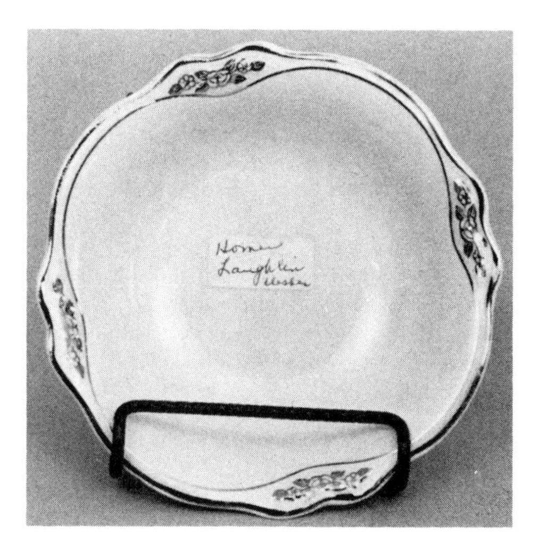

Illegible price tags are confusing and useless. Your customer might be able to figure out the first two words are "Homer Laughlin," but he'll scratch his head a few times before he deciphers the third word, "Dishes."

The Key to Better Tags

Does the phrase "chicken scratches" come to mind when you think of your handwriting? Is your illegible writing costing you sales? Consider typing your price tags. Manual typewriters can be purchased at yard sales, flea markets, and auctions for next to nothing. An electric typewriter will cost more, but the quality of the lettering may be worth the added expense. Computer-generated price tags are another option. Whether creating your own format or filling in the blanks on a pre-printed sticker, your tags will look professional and will be easy to read.

When it is necessary to include cents, write the tag so dollars and cents are separate entities. If your Matchbox Rolls-Royce is $17.50, write the 17 in larger numbers and underline the 50 to set it apart.

Unless you are using tags with pre-printed dollar signs, always put a dollar sign before the price. Otherwise, your customer might think the price is a booth number, an inventory number, or some irrelevant figure. Print your dollar signs neatly and make sure the vertical slash is where it belongs. If you use two slashes and one drifts toward the price, it could be mistaken as a "1." Your customer might assume your castor set is tagged $195 rather than $95.

When making price tags, avoid using cursive, no matter how neatly you write. Others may find it difficult to read. Instead, print as neatly as

▶ FYI

You know your price tags are illegible when:

1 People mistake your handwriting for another language.
2 Mall employees often leave notes asking you to "please decipher" tag descriptions.
3 Tags look better when you take *off* your glasses.
4 The Antiques Police frequently cite you for illegible tags.
5 Concerned customers ask how long you've been suffering from palsy.
6 Your tags look like they were written during a roller coaster ride.
7 The CIA recruits you as a cryptographer.
8 People ask if you wish you were ambidextrous since it's obvious you've injured you writing hand.
9 Customers often mumble to themselves that they need their vision checked.
10 Your handwriting is featured on an episode of "Unsolved Mysteries."

FYI

Dealers whose handwritten price tags exhibit a certain *je ne sairs quoi*:

Movers—They never seem to know which end is up. Information is placed haphazardly on the tag, sometimes moving up and down, and sometimes from side to side.

Shakers—They write so poorly you'd swear they must live over the ever-active San Andreas fault and write while gyrating to Elvis tunes.

Scribblers—They always got low grades in penmanship. You can't tell if the tag reads "Schoenhut Hippo" or "Dead Se Scrolls."

Scratchers—They believe it's necessary to give a Rorschach test to every customer. Blunders are scratched out, leaving a series of inkblots ready to be analyzed.

Shrinkers—They could write the Gettysburg Address on the head of a pin. You need a magnifying glass to read their small print.

Enlargers—They write tags that can be seen from outer space. Shuttle astronauts have no problem reading these large-print editions.

Crammers—They subscribe to the nineteen-clowns-in-a-Volkswagen method of writing tags, believing there's always room for more information.

Abbreviators—They write everything in code and can find a way to shorten any work: "rd. gl. bwl. gr. dep." Red glaring bowlers greeting deputies?" you ask. No, "Round glass bowl—green depression."

possible. Your efforts will be appreciated by the customer as well as the clerk who writes the sales ticket.

Also, separate the various units of information on your price tags. You don't want customers to think your booth number is the price. Pre-printed tags eliminate much of the confusion. Widely used in antique malls, they have individual sections for booth number, price, item description, and inventory number.

45 Provide Descriptions and Information

YOUR TAGS ARE TALKING.

There's a silent salesman on your showroom floor. He's giving your customers information about your merchandise. What they're learning can make or break a sale. Only you can control this mute middleman.

Who is this salesperson? He's the merchandise description you write on every price tag. Make sure those descriptions provide relevant, correct information about the piece. It's their job to promote items in the absence of a sales clerk.

The small size of most price tags will limit the length of your descriptions. Use the space wisely. Don't waste the customer's time with frivolous information. It's good to note that your dog figural napkin ring was made by Reed and Barton; but there's no need to say the dog resembles Lassie.

Also, avoid sounding condescending. There's no need to write "glass bowl"—the customer has already figured that out. A better description might be "10-inch Fostoria American bowl." Impress the buyer with your knowledge. You might provide historical background, give dates, or list the type of wood.

Descriptions need to be just that: *descriptive.* One common mistake is to tag a piece of artwork "signed." Go a step further. Tell your customer who signed the work. A collector looking for watercolors by a particular artist might miss the signature on your painting. If so, you'll miss the sale. Give him the information he wants on the price tag and you'll not have to worry about who's missing what.

Those Three Little Words

Although your price tags should be as descriptive as possible, try to avoid the following adjectives:

Old People browsing in an antique shop expect the merchandise to be old. There's no need to reiterate the point. Instead, tell your customers how old an item is—that your Teco vase is circa 1910–1922 or that your Ingersoll Mickey Mouse wrist watch was made in the 1930s.

Rare This is a relative term which has been cheapened by overuse. If you can prove rarity, do so. Describe your wooden rooster apple peeler as one-of-a-kind or your special-edition plate as one of only 50 produced.

Very Delete this word from your vocabulary. It adds nothing but hype to your descriptions, especially when paired with "old" and "rare."

When necessary, provide additional information on a shelf-talker. You might want to note that your Civil War saber was used at both Gettysburg and Antietam and that papers of authentication are located at the front desk. Those details might be the extra nudge needed to sell the piece. Remember, the more a person knows about your merchandise, the more comfortable he will feel buying it.

Good descriptions can actually help increase the turnover rate of your merchandise. One dealer's pine dometop trunk with dovetailed construction was a good buy at only $65, yet the piece went unsold for nearly three months. Then the dealer changed the description on the price tag, adding "dovetailed" in front of "pine trunk." An enthusiastic customer bought the trunk three days later.

Bad descriptions, like poor customer service, can cost you money. In one shop, a custard glass creamer and sugar from a popular health resort had a single price tag of $50. The dealer became outraged when a customer asked if $50 was his best price for the pair. "The pair?" the dealer snapped. "They're $50 apiece. I can't afford to sell them both for $50." Needless to say, the dealer lost both the sale and the future business of that customer. His misleading price tag and rude behavior guaranteed the customer would not return.

Inadequate descriptions can cost you money. These three items might seem particularly unassuming, especially if your price tags simply identify them as a bean pot, a sketch, and a tile. However, your customer might take a second look when you tell him more about the pieces. Drop a few names. These items are actually a Fulper bean pot, an Otto Stark pencil sketch, and a 1953 Rookwood tile.

Stuffed. Steiff. What's the Difference?

Your merchandise might be throwing hints your way. You had better pay attention or you'll be throwing money away.

That's what happened to one dealer who priced a toy fish $18 and labeled it "stuffed fish." However, a button in the fin verified the toy was a piece of Steiff. Either the dealer hadn't fully examined the fish, or he wasn't knowledgeable about stuffed animals. Had he researched his merchandise and then promoted it properly, he could have increased his profit.

Another dealer tagged a Mission-style table $45 and labeled it "lamp table." However, the bottom of the piece carried a more descriptive name: Stickley. The dealer lost hundreds of dollars because he didn't thoroughly examine the piece.

You can't fully describe your merchandise if you don't know what it is. Be as knowledgeable as possible. Do some research when necessary. And, easiest of all, inspect every item. You might be surprised by what you find.

Just another stuffed toy? Not quite. Notice the button in the fin? This fish is actually a piece of Steiff.

Descriptions on price tags are particularly important at antique malls. Provide enough basic information that a clerk can determine when tags have been switched by an unscrupulous customer. Switch-proof tags require specific descriptions on every piece. "Roseville Freesia basket, 8 inches, $85" is a thorough tag for a piece of pottery. But, if your child's wicker Easter basket is simply tagged "Basket, $10," you're inviting trouble. If someone places the $10 tag on your Roseville piece, a clerk may not know anything is amiss. Fully describe all your merchandise, no matter how ordinary it may be.

46 Tell the Truth

THE TRUTH, THE WHOLE TRUTH, AND NOTHING BUT THE TRUTH.

It's a popular piece of American folklore. A young George Washington and a freshly felled cherry tree. An ax and an admission. "I cannot tell a lie," declared the future Father of Our Country. The rest, as they say, is history.

Honesty is still the best policy, particularly when it comes to dealing with your customers. Shoppers are more likely to patronize reputable dealers. Disclose everything you know about a piece, even the bad. Point out that your Mettlach stein has a cracked handle. Inform the customer that your decorated blanket chest has had two feet replaced or that a Mocha Ware pitcher has been professionally repaired. Be upfront. Note damage and repairs on the price tag.

One sure way to destroy your reputation is to sell merchandise that your customer later learns is damaged or repaired. If he bought your Essolube advertising puzzle, believing it was complete, you'll probably lose his business when he discovers three pieces are missing. He'll tell his friends about the dirty, lying, no-good dealer who sold him the puzzle. You'll lose their business, too.

In noting flaws, correctly describe the extent of the damage. Don't label your Hubley motorcycle "touched up" if it's been completely repainted. Likewise, don't say your Blue Willow teapot has a "chigger bite" if there's a fingernail-sized chunk out of the lid. One show dealer had a particularly hard time with this concept, tagging a two-gallon Red Wing crock "rare

Chip Off the Old Block

One dealer at an antique mall offered a large selection of art pottery, most of which had chips or hairlines. He admitted he had a lot of flawed merchandise, yet none of the price tags noted any damage.

He didn't care about detailing the damage, but it mattered to his customers. They noticed it. And, they didn't like what they saw.

After examining a number of nicked and cracked items, customers assumed every piece of pottery was damaged. Even the seemingly perfect pieces were suspect. Hesitant to get stuck with an imperfect item, customers walked away without making a purchase.

size, hairlines." In fact, the piece was common, and the cracks were large enough to ride a moped through.

Likewise, be honest when describing the condition of an item. "Mint" means it's like-new. Use the term only when appropriate. A dealer at one top-quality antique show offered a "mint condition" canning jar with three chips on the inside lip. The century-old jar was in good shape, but it was far from mint.

Circumstances that aren't necessarily your fault can come back to haunt you. One dealer sold a dry sink which was infested with powder-post beetles. The price reflected the damage, but the infestation was neither noted on the tag nor explained to the customer. Only after he got the piece home did the buyer discover the insect damage. He returned to the dealer, demanding a refund. The dealer refused, claiming the customer should have examined the dry sink before he bought it.

Who's at fault here? Both parties. The buyer should have inspected the dry sink before purchasing it, and the dealer should have noted the damage before the piece was sold.

If your customer asks a question about a piece of merchandise, and you don't know the answer, just say so. Tell him you will try to obtain the information—then do it. Don't bluff. People don't necessarily expect you to know everything, but they do expect you to tell the truth and carry through on what you promise.

Note any merchandise damage, and make sure you do so honestly. Obviously, these two pieces are badly cracked and flaking. State that on the price tag. A customer will question your integrity if these items are described as having "hairlines" and "some glaze imperfections."

VI Cleanliness

Take your most unusual item and make it the focal point of a striking display. Then stand back as interested customers gaze in awe. Add a full ashtray, a couple of wadded up tissues, some potato chip crumbs, a half-eaten apple, and a few hungry ants. Notice the difference?

Customers expect cleanliness. When they walk into your shop, they like to know the floors have been swept, the shelves have been dusted, and the litter has been picked up. If your shop is untidy, they'll think you just don't care.

Cleanliness goes beyond your booth. It also includes your merchandise. If your folk art birdhouse is covered with pigeon droppings, even the hardiest of collectors will be hesitant to handle the piece. Show your customers you're concerned with the appearance of your merchandise. If you come clean with your merchandise, you're more likely to make a tidy profit.

47 Tidy Your Booth

IT'S A DIRTY JOB, BUT SOMEONE'S GOT TO DO IT.

The booth looked as if the owner only cleaned on the fourth Sunday of every month beginning with the letter J. The words "dust me" were traced on a Queen Anne drop-leaf table, and an overflowing ashtray rested on the showcase. An empty soda can sat in the middle of a display of mantel clocks, a collection of dead bugs was on the windowsill, and the floor hadn't been swept in weeks.

Not a pretty sight.

Ideally, your booth should be cleaned at least once a week. If you aren't already there that often to check your merchandise, you probably aren't doing enough. And, as most dealers know, there's plenty to do.

Welcome to Boothkeeping 101.

It's a four-letter word, but it's still the operative word: *dust!* The majority of dealers overlook this chore. "But," you ask, "do customers really notice?" Yes, they certainly do. Many even expect that when they pick up an American Sweetheart tumbler, a dust ring will show them exactly where to replace it.

It doesn't matter that you might not have the time to dust. All your customer knows is that you didn't *make* time to dust. Even if the rest of your booth is free of trash and the floors are relatively clean, dusty shelves and dusty merchandise are a sure sign that you just don't care.

It's when they pick up that American Sweetheart tumbler and *don't* see any dust that they know you care enough about your booth and your merchandise to undertake the ardurous task of dusting. They will assume that if you're concerned about the condition of your booth, you're probably concerned about their business, too.

▶ FYI

Essential cleaning supplies:

1. Dust cloths
2. Small paintbrush (for dusting smalls)
3. Feather duster (for when you're short on time)
4. Glass cleaner
5. All-purpose cleaner
6. Cleaning rags
7. Newspapers (for cleaning glass)
8. Broom or dust mop
9. Vacuum cleaner
10. Hand vac (for small messes or upholstery)

More than just dusting needs to be done, however. Play litter police. Check crocks, baskets, and dishes for trash customers may have left behind. You can't control their inconsiderate actions, but it does reflect negatively on you when the rest of you customers see a Snickers wrapper on the floor or an empty McDonald's cup on a shelf.

Also check for smokers' debris. Empty and clean ashtrays frequently. Don't forget to check for ashes and butts in other places. Your Jadite mixing bowls, your Captain Kangaroo cup, or even your hardwood floor might have been used as an ashtray by some unthinking customer.

Playing janitor is a necessary part of your job. Shoppers are more likely to focus on your merchandise once the trash has been removed from your booth. In this case, the litter included a used tissue, a coffee cup, a full ashtray, a Sprite can, some candy wrappers, and a collection of cigarette butts in a piece of merchandise.

Litter Never Sleeps

The high volume of traffic generated by shows or flea markets means you must frequently check your booth for litter. You may get tired of cleaning up after everyone, but the customer who walks into your booth at 4:45 in the afternoon is seeing it for the first time. He doesn't care that people have been in and out since six o'clock that morning. No excuses allowed. He expects the same consideration you showed your early-morning customers—a neat and orderly booth.

Don't contribute to the litter problem. If you offer complimentary candy, provide a trash container for wrappers. Likewise, store your cleaning supplies out of sight.

Several other important tasks can be performed while you are cleaning your booth. Check to see what items have been moved and which are still in the same spot as your last visit. This tells you what merchandise your customers are interested in. If your oyster tins haven't been touched, it might be time to replace them with other merchandise. If your fruit jars are always a mess, you can assume customers are looking at them. Create a special display to take advantage of that interest.

Also use your cleaning time to make sure sets of items are complete. You may discover that one of your aluminum tumblers has been separated

▶ FYI

Don't forget:

1 If you have mirrors—whether merchandise or props—be sure to remove fingerprints.
2 Dust more than just the tops of merchandise and display fixtures. Also get the sides, bottoms, stretchers, etc.
3 Dust inside showcases. Don't incorrectly assume dust doesn't accumulate there.
4 Dust light fixtures and bulbs.
5 Empty and clean ashtrays.
6 Check crocks, baskets, vases, bowls, etc. for trash.
7 Sweep and vacuum.
8 Remove cobwebs from ceilings and walls. Be sure to check sides and bases of display fixtures—areas that tend to be forgotten.
9 Clean dead insects out of corners, windowsills, and merchandise.
10 Remove stains. Some clumsy customer may have spilled his chocolate milkshake on your carpet.

from the the other five pieces in the set. If the tag says "set of 6," your customer may lose interest when he can find only five tumblers. Take a few seconds to regroup your merchandise.

While cleaning, check for items that are missing. One dealer offered a graniteware cup with a soldier motif. The price tag read "Child's cup and plate, $6." However, the plate wasn't in the booth. Few customers would consider paying the full price for just the cup. Assuming the plate had been stolen, the dealer should have retagged the cup at a lower price.

If you don't police your booth you'll not know when items have been shoplifted. Your pewter spoon mold might have been filched days ago, but you may not discover it's missing until three weeks from now, when it's not included in your sales tickets.

You can even look for trends in shoplifting activity. If you're losing a toothpick holder every couple of weeks, someone may be stealing your merchandise on the installment plan. Maybe it's time to put those items in a locked showcase instead of on a shelf.

Cleaning your booth may seem like a monumental task. And, it is—when it's done infrequently. Avoid the once-a-week, all-day cleaning marathon by doing a little every day or so.

48 Clean Your Merchandise

RUB A DUB DUB, IT'S TIME FOR A SCRUB.

The dealer holding the Rookwood vase was on the verge of making a decision—buy the piece or pass. He turned the vase over, re-examined the mark, and double-checked the price. Still unsure. He looked inside the piece, scraped some lime deposits with his fingernail, and looked at the price again. He frowned, glanced inside the vase one last time, set it back on the shelf, and walked away.

It was a close call. He liked the vase, and the price wasn't bad, but the lime deposits were enough to make him forgo the sale. He later told the mall manager, "I would have bought that piece of Rookwood if it'd been clean inside. But, for that kind of money, I don't want to have to mess with it."

Although the vase was free of dirt, the lime hadn't been removed. Some vinegar, a bottle brush, and a little bit of work could have saved the sale.

It's a lesson worth remembering. Clean merchandise sells more readily than dirty merchandise. You may have creative displays, but they'll look second-rate if your merchandise isn't spotless.

Most shoppers are looking for items they can immediately use. Your merchandise should be clean and ready to go. Wash your milk glass hen-on-nest, put a fresh coat of paste wax on your walnut bucket bench, and brush the dust and straw off your cast-iron Deere & Co. implement seat.

Always remove sticker residue. Gummy, dirty adhesive from previous tags tells the customer you're not overly concerned with how your merchandise looks.

A dealer at one posh metropolitan antique show went to great lengths to present the perfect booth. He used moveable walls and colorful carpets to create eye-catching room settings. Quality accessories complimented his

Play Mr. Clean

Spotless merchandise not only presents a positive image to customers, it also allows you to increase your profits. Shoppers will be willing to spend more for a clean item than for one which is dirty. You might be able to get only $4 for your Fire-King plate if it looks like it's been in a barn since the last moon walk. But, when cleaned, that same plate could bring $5. A little soap and water can really make a difference when your customer is deciding how much the piece is worth to him.

early American furniture. His *piece de resistance* was an outstanding selection of framed wildlife and botanical prints. Unfortunately, that's where the display fell flat. One of the prints had pieces of two old price tags stuck to the glass. Another was smudged where a sticker had been removed. This carelessness ruined the professional image the dealer worked so hard to create.

Often, the problem involves more than just sticker residue. The entire item might be dirty, and a cursory wash just isn't going to cut it. As your mother used to say, "Don't forget to scrub behind your ears!" Apply that same advice to your merchandise. When necessary, use a toothbrush and non-abrasive cleanser to get the grime out of cracks and crevices.

However, cleaning your merchandise before putting it on display doesn't mean your work is done. Expect the unexpected and frequently check your merchandise. You might find that someone has dripped strawberry ice cream on your Russel Wright divided relish, spilled root beer on your Flower Garden quilt, or stuck a wad of chewing gum under the top of your tiger maple one-drawer stand.

In addition, make sure customers haven't left trash behind. You might discover someone has hidden a pop can in your copper teakettle, deposited an old tissue in your Dr Pepper fountain glass, or used your Waterford pitcher as an ashtray.

Also check for dead insects in your merchandise. Nothing does a better job of convincing your customer you never clean or stock your booth. The one-time customer might be bothered by the dead cockroach in your box of Hall Crocus dinnerware. The frequent customer will be particularly annoyed when he sees that bug for three weeks.

That's a Wrap!

Your concern for cleanliness shouldn't stop when the customer brings an item to the cash register. Wrap and pack each purchase so it will remain clean on the trip home, whether the customer is going around the block or across the country.

Be particularly careful when wrapping merchandise in newsprint. Your customer won't be too pleased if he gets home and finds ink on his newly purchased homespun pillow cases or bisque Donald Duck figurine. Wrap light-colored items in tissue or put them in a sack. If necessary, you can then wrap the package in newspaper for extra protection.

One antique mall uses the end rolls from its local newspaper to wrap purchases. This uninked newsprint comes on a long tube and can be cut to the desired size. Another mall recycles foam packing sheets discarded by a local furniture dealer.

Naturally, clean merchandise is more appealing. Notice the difference in these displays after the doily was ironed, the merchandise was washed, and the dead bugs were discarded.

You should clean all your merchandise, regardless of its value. However, you'll seem especially uncaring if your big-ticket items are dirty. At one antique show, a $495 Van Briggle vase was caked with dust and had grime in the crevices of the design. A thorough cleaning would have made the piece more presentable, increasing the likelihood it would sell.

VII Useful Records

As a dealer, buying and selling antiques and collectibles is a business. If you are going to function as a business person, you must keep good records.

At a minimum, a good bookkeeping system should provide you with quick access to information about your merchandise. You might need to know how much you paid for your leather firefighter's helmet or where you stored your Tarzan comic books. Thorough records will show that you paid $75 for the helmet and your comics are stored in the hall closet.

Records can also reveal buying trends. A logbook might tell you that out-of-state dealers are buying oak furniture in the fall and local shoppers are looking for wicker in the spring. Take advantage of this information. Highlight those types of merchandise during the appropriate seasons.

49 Keep Inventories and Logbooks

GUINNESS MIGHT NOT CARE, BUT YOU SHOULD.

Your house resembles a war zone. You can't find the stereographs you bought for resale last summer. You've looked through the boxes at the top of the stairwell. You've checked the guest room closet. You've even searched the junk drawer in the kitchen. All to no avail. Maybe you gave them away as Christmas presents or traded them for some advertising punchboards. You're just not sure. At this rate, you'll find them about the time Halley's Comet returns.

There's got to be a better way.

There is. Keep an inventory.

A comprehensive inventory provides important information about your business. It can help you locate those missing stereographs. In addition, it can tell you which types of merchandise are selling and which pieces have been on display too long. If souvenir spoons generally sell within three weeks of being logged in your inventory, you'll know you've got a pool of eager buyers. But, if your charge coins are still in the showcase ten months later, you'll think twice before purchasing additional ones for resale. Keep track of when you put an item in your booth and when it sells. You'll better understand what shoppers are buying.

Check for theft by periodically comparing your inventory list with your merchandise. You might spot a trend. If three tin cookie cutters have been stolen during the past six weeks, you'll want to consider moving those items to a safer location, such as a locked showcase.

To be effective an inventory must be detailed. It will do you little good if items are simply listed as "in storage." That could mean any one of 40 boxes in your attic. Avoid the frustration and save yourself some time by using a comprehensive storage plan. Number your boxes and itemize the contents. Transfer that information to your inventory. When you need your Norman Rockwell Christmas plate, you'll know it's in Box #14.

Your inventory should provide an overall accounting of your merchandise. Information should include when and where an item was bought, its purchase price, and its current location. You'll also want to know when and where an item was sold, its selling price, and your gross profit or loss.

Another way to learn about the market is to keep a logbook. Track factors such as weather and special events that can affect your business. Spurts in sales might make sense when your logbook tells you a game collector's convention was in town, a tour group stopped at your mall, or

> **FYI**
>
> Categories for your inventory:
>
> 1. Code number
> 2. Item description
> 3. Date purchased
> 4. Where purchased
> 5. Purchase price
> 6. Current location
> 7. Date placed in mall or shop
> 8. Date sold
> 9. Where sold
> 10. Selling price
> 11. Gross profit/loss

the local Blueberry Festival was under way. You might also discover that jardinieres sell extremely well in the spring but not in the fall. Plan your displays accordingly.

Computers are a godsend when it comes to keeping records. If you've never used one, don't panic. Many computers and software packages are user-friendly. In addition to keeping records, computers can be used to create tags and signs, print invoices and receipts, and handle correspondence.

50 Finalize the Sale

"Y'ALL COME BACK NOW, YA HEAR?"

The need for a professional image doesn't end when the customer hands you a piece of merchandise and reaches for his wallet. You still have work to do. Speak to him in a genuine, friendly tone and use his name if possible. When appropriate, make positive comments about his purchases. If you think the Edison phonograph is a particularly good buy, tell him so.

Remember, he isn't leaving with just his purchase. He'll be taking paperwork with him. Make sure the receipt represents your business in a positive light. The forms you use should mirror your professional image. They must be neat, orderly, and complete, whether purchased at a local business store or custom-made on your home computer.

A receipt serves as the only permanent record of the sales transaction. Make sure it contains all the information you or your customer might need. Show the name, address, and telephone number of your shop or mall. Record the date, a description of the item, and the price. Also note the method of payment and whether the bill is paid-in-full. If the sale involves any special details, such as delivery instructions, include them as well.

Layaway forms are similar to sales receipts, but should also contain the terms of the layaway and the customer's name, address, and telephone number. After your customer reads and understands the terms, ask him to sign the form. One copy should be given to your customer, one copy

Counter Intelligence

Counting back change is a lost art in today's business world, yet it's a great customer service tool. There's no better way to assure both you and the customer that the correct amount of change was received.

Two figures are used to determine the amount of change a customer is due: the sales total and the amount of cash tendered. If a customer purchases your rabbit hand puppet for $11.33 and pays with a $50 bill, he should receive $38.67 in change.

"Your total was $11.33," you would begin. Now, count back the change. Start with the smallest denomination and move to the largest. Pennies first. Count the pennies, one at a time, and hand them to the customer as you add them to the total. "$11.34, $11.35." Nickels next. "$11.40." Then the dimes. "$11.50." Finally, the quarters. "$11.75, $12." Now it's time for the paper money. Again, count from the smallest denomination to the largest. First, hand him the ones. "$13, $14, $15." Then a five. "$20." A ten. "$30." And, a twenty. "$50."

It's that easy!

> **▶ FYI**
>
> What the well-dressed receipt is wearing:
>
> 1. Shop name, address, and telephone number
> 2. Sales clerk
> 3. Date of purchase
> 4. Item description
> 5. Original price
> 6. Discount
> 7. Subtotal
> 8. Tax
> 9. Total
> 10. Type of payment
> 11. "Paid-in-Full"
>
> Additional information for tax-exempt purchases:
>
> 12. Business name, address, and telephone number
> 13. Buyer's name and title
> 14. Signature
> 15. Purchaser's tax number

should be kept for your files, and one copy should remain with the merchandise until it is picked up.

If possible, keep all your layaway merchandise in one special area. You'll know where to find your customer's spinning wheel when he comes to pay it off. If you cannot place layaways in a separate spot, prevent future confusion by noting their location on the layaway form.

Make sure you and your employees can properly finalize every type of sale. Know where all the necessary forms are located and be able to complete them. If a worker isn't sure what to do when a customer uses his Visa card to buy a jacquard coverlet, the entire organization will seem incompetent.

You should also learn the tax laws and have the appropriate tax-exempt forms on hand. If a tax form must be filed for a new dealer, save time by having him complete it while you're writing the receipt.

> **▶ FYI**
>
> Layaway forms should contain the following information:
>
> 1. Buyer's name, address, and telephone number
> 2. Item description
> 3. Price
> 4. Discount
> 5. Subtotal
> 6. Tax
> 7. Total
> 8. Down payment
> 9. Balance due
> 10. Length of layaway
> 11. Payment dates

After you have written the receipt, let your customer know the total. Don't just slide the receipt across the counter and expect him to figure it out for himself. Tell him. Nicely.

Preserve your professional image by counting back your customer's change. This guarantees you'll give him the correct amount and shows him you are as concerned about his money as he is.

Finally, smile and warmly thank the customer for his patronage.

Index